Warrior • 116

Viet Cong Fighter

Gordon L Rottman • Illustrated by Howard Gerrard

First published in Great Britain in 2007 by Osprey Publishing,
Midland House, West Way, Botley, Oxford OX2 0PH, UK
443 Park Avenue South, New York, NY 10016, USA
E-mail: info@ospreypublishing.com

A CIP catalog record for this book is available from the British Library

ISBN: 978 1 84603 126 7

Page layout by: Mark Holt
Typeset in Helvetica Neue and ITC New Baskerville
Index by Alison Worthington
Originated by PDQ Digital Media Solutions
Printed in China through Worldprint

07 08 09 10 11   10 9 8 7 6 5 4 3 2 1

FOR A CATALOG OF ALL BOOKS PUBLISHED BY OSPREY MILITARY AND
AVIATION PLEASE CONTACT:

NORTH AMERICA
Osprey Direct, c/o Random House Distribution Center, 400 Hahn Road,
Westminster, MD 21157
E-mail: info@ospreydirect.com

ALL OTHER REGIONS
Osprey Direct UK, P.O. Box 140 Wellingborough, Northants, NN8 2FA, UK
E-mail: info@ospreydirect.co.uk

www.ospreypublishing.com

Artist's note

Readers may care to note that the original paintings from
which the color plates in this book were prepared are
available for private sale. All reproduction copyright
whatsoever is retained by the Publishers. All inquiries
should be addressed to:

Howard Gerrard
11 Oaks Road
Tenterden
Kent
TN30 6RD
UK

The Publishers regret that they can enter into no
correspondence upon this matter.

Acknowledgments

The author is indebted to Steve Sherman, Bill Laurie,
William Howard, and Paul Lemmer for their assistance in
providing information and materials.

Editor's note

Vietnamese accents have not been used in this book.
Unless otherwise stated, all images are in the public domain.

Abbreviations

ARVN	Army of the Republic of Vietnam (pronounced "are-van")
CIDG	Civilian Irregular Defense Force
DKZ	*Dai-bac Khong Ziat* (recoilless rifle)
DRV	Democratic Republic of Vietnam (North Vietnam)
GPA	Guerrilla Popular Army
NLF	National Liberation Front
NVA	North Vietnamese Army
PAVN	People's Army of Vietnam (NLF armed forces – VC)
PF	Popular Force
PLA	People's LIberation Army (Viet Cong)
PRG	Provisional Revolutionary Government
PRP	People's Revolutionary Party
RDC	Rural Development Cadre
RF	Regional Force
RVN	Republic of Vietnam (South Vietnam)
RPG	Rocket-propelled grenade (RPG-2, RPG-7 – aka B40, B41)
VC	Viet Cong
VCI	Viet Cong Infrastructure

Front cover: Local Force Viet Cong transit a Mekong Delta canal aboard
sanpans, a primary means of of moving personnel and supplies. (Topfoto)

CONTENTS

INTRODUCTION   4
Liberate the South

CHRONOLOGY   8

ORGANIZATION   8
PLA forces • The cadre • Guerrilla Popular Army

RECRUITMENT   11

TRAINING   14
Indoctrination

APPEARANCE   18
Local Forces • Main Forces

WEAPONS AND EQUIPMENT   20

CONDITIONS OF SERVICE   30

BELIEF AND BELONGING   44
Confucianism • Communism • The rules of the party

EXPERIENCE IN BATTLE   49
Special Attack Corps

AFTERMATH OF BATTLE   58

COLLECTIONS, MUSEUMS, AND REENACTMENT   59

BIBLIOGRAPHY   60

COLOR PLATE COMMENTARY   61

INDEX   64

VIET CONG FIGHTER

INTRODUCTION

There are many myths and misconceptions surrounding the Viet Cong, who have become the shadowy warriors of the Vietnam War. The popular image of them dressed in black pajamas, rising up and fighting a relentless and brutal terror campaign is not unfounded, but it is not the whole picture.

The Viet Cong (VC) were the communist insurgents of South Vietnam – the Republic of Vietnam (RVN). They were citizens of the RVN, and their effort to overthrow the legal government of the RVN was supported by North Vietnam – the Democratic Republic of Vietnam (DRV), and its People's Army of Vietnam (Quan Doi Dang Dan, or PAVN), more commonly known as the North Vietnamese Army (NVA).

Army of the Republic of Vietnam (ARVN) troops search a shell-battered village. Some VC had served in the ARVN while others joined various Vietnamese paramilitary and security organizations for training, but mainly to pilfer weapons and supplies, subvert soldiers, and collect intelligence.

The NVA was important to the VC. They could not have survived without its support, which came in the form of leadership cadres, both military and political, arms, supplies, and training. The NVA in turn also relied on the VC for intelligence, guides, and locally procured supplies and services. In 1964 battered VC units were already receiving NVA fillers. After the tremendous losses of the 1968 Tet Offensive, most VC units contained more NVA than VC, often up to 80–90 percent. A large percentage of the NVA were members of the Vietnam Workers' Party (Dang Lao Dong Viet Nam), the DRV Communist Party known simply as the "Lao Dong."

Some people like to point out that the term "Viet Cong" is incorrect. On one level this is true. The National Front for the Liberation of South Vietnam (Mat tran Dan toc Giai phong mien Nam Viet Nam), or the National Liberation Front (NLF), was both a political organization with its own government superimposed on South Vietnam and an armed insurgent force. Its military arm was the People's Liberation Armed Forces (Quan Doi Giai Phong Nhan Dan, or PLAF) or more commonly, the People's Liberation Army (Quan Doi Giai Phong, or PLA). To the South Vietnamese, civilian and military, the Free World forces, the public at large, and, as the author knows firsthand, to the PLA itself, they were commonly known as the "Viet Cong" or VC, a contraction of Dang Viet Nam Cong San (Vietnamese Communist Party).

The American soldier called them the "VC," "Victor Charlie," or simply "Charlie" or the "Cong." Some writers have recently claimed that Charlie is a derogatory term in the grunt's vocabulary. However, it is actually a neutral term and nothing more than the phonetic alphabet word for the "C" in VC. Likewise, the terms "Charles" and "Chuck" were occasionally also used as nicknames. If "Charlie" was meant to be demeaning then grunts would not have called their enemy "Mr. Charles" or "Sir Charles." The grunt had other names for the VC which were certainly meant to degrade: "gook," "dink," "slope," "slope-head," "zip," or "zipper-head," the same terms unfortunately applied to Vietnamese civilians.

As individual fighters, the VC referred to themselves as "combatant" or "soldier" (*chien si*) or "liberation fighter" (*thu chien*). They could be inventive, ingenious, and crafty, but they also made their share of mistakes and miscalculations. Many operations were executed masterfully. These were sometimes entirely successful or were defeated by massive firepower and well-maneuvered opponents, regardless of how expertly planned and executed they were. In other instances the fighters made stupid mistakes and acted illogically. There were units which were resolute and willing to die in-place, others panicked and fled. It was not uncommon for Americans to admire their proficiency one day and the next to ask, after an obvious blunder, "What were they thinking?" Overall, however, they demonstrated a high degree of perseverance, endurance, and dedication to their cause.

Here Main Force fighters fire a 7.62mm SG-43 (Chinese Type 53) heavy machine gun from an antiaircraft mount during Tet 1968. Note the North Vietnamese-made entrenching tool. (Central Press/Getty Images)

The VC undertook a major effort to disrupt the Vietnamese transportation system. By 1962 the rail system was virtually destroyed and unusable. It was not until 1969 that lengthy rail sections began to be reopened.

Liberate the South

"Release the South" (*Giai phong mien Nam*) was the theme song of the NLF, whose goal was to the "free the people" (*Nhan Dan*). Written in 1961, the song was adopted as the national anthem of the Provisional Revolutionary Government of the Republic of South Vietnam (Chinh Phu Cach Mang Lam Thoi Cong Hoa Mien Nam Viet Nam, or PRG), the NLF's "shadow government," on June 8, 1969. The official mission statement of the NLF was: to free South Vietnam of its imperialistic, democratic government through an armed struggle (*dau tranh va trang*) known as the People's War – a Chinese-influenced concept of revolutionary warfare. The NLF adhered to a Marxist-Leninist ideology shaped by Ho Chi Minh, also known as Bac Ho (Uncle Ho), the president of North Vietnam. The flaw in the NLF's goal was that it relied heavily on North Vietnam. While there was talk of "reunification" of north and south, the two nations had never been really unified to begin with.

French Indochina had been a collection of colonies and protectorates: Laos, Cambodia, Cochinchine, Annam, and Tonkin. With the ousting of the French in 1954, Tonkin and part of Annam became North Vietnam and the rest of Annam and Cochinchine went to South Vietnam. Ethnically and linguistically, the North, Central, and South Vietnamese people are different. North Vietnam had no intention of allowing the NLF to play any part in a unified Vietnam. The NLF and the PLA were merely tools of the northerners.

The NLF was formed on December 20, 1960, mainly from members of the League for the Independence of Vietnam (Viet Nam Doc Lap Dong Minh Hoi, or Vietminh). In October 1959 the Vietminh and Communist Party were outlawed by the Saigon government. Many Vietminh moved north after 1954 to be absorbed into the NVA. More remained in the south to carry on a "political struggle," but North Vietnam changed this to an "armed struggle" in January 1959. Between 1959 and 1964 80,000 southern-born NVA were sent south as recruiting cadres.

To confuse the issue another organization was established on January 1 1962, the People's Revolutionary Party (Dang Nhan Dan Cach mang Viet Nam, or PRP). While the PRP claimed it was separate from the vanguard of the NLF, the two organizations' headquarters were co-located in Binh

In what the VC called "liberated areas," the people were encouraged and "guided" to participate in community work projects. Some of these were for the common good, like cleaning out a silted irrigation ditch. More often they dug field fortifications and produced booby trap components. For digging, this type of large-bladed hoe was more common than the shovel.

Duong Province (War Zone D) with elements in Tay Ninh Province. The PRP was merely an extension of North Vietnam's Lao Dong Party. The NLF in theory controlled the PLA and coordinated the activities of the PRP through the Central Office, South Vietnam (COSVN), which later operated from Cambodia. Military operations of both the PLA and NVA were directed from Hanoi.

The NLF had a long-established "shadow government," called the Viet Cong Infrastructure (VCI) by Free World forces. They had their own administrative boundaries dissecting the country with a complex and changing structure of inter-zones and zones, provincial and district political headquarters (central committees) and military headquarters (these operated as two separate, but mutually supporting headquarters). The NLF collected taxes, attempted to control the population with varying degrees of success, made efforts to hamper local RVN government authorities, and executed military operations. At the village level there were the administrative and political cadres, which formed the liberation committees. There were also liberation associations, clubs of a sort, designed to educate and motivate the people. These included: Farmer's, Worker's, Student's Youth, Women's, and Cultural Liberation associations and other socio-political organizations.

The PRG was formally established on June 8, 1969 after the failed 1968 Tet Offensive. This event saw the general abandonment of the People's War concept in an attempt to show that the offensive had been more successful than it actually was. The PRG was also keen to show that the NLF was composed mainly of southerners, when in fact much of the PLA's strength was in NVA regulars, who lived in anticipation of the final victory and the expectation that the NLF would be included in the unified government. The PRG were keen to show that the revolutionary struggle in the South had broader support than it actually did. The top PRG officials and ministers operated in exile inside Laos and later Cambodia, driven farther away by the US offensive into Cambodia in 1970. Even though the VCI had spread through much of the RVN countryside, the PRG offered little real challenge to the Saigon government. It required a large-scale conventional invasion of the South, a country later abandoned by the United States, to overthrow Saigon.

CHRONOLOGY

February 12, 1955 First US military advisors arrive in RVN.

July 21, 1955 Vietnam divided at the 17th Parallel as the French withdraw.

January 1959 North Vietnam issues resolution changing its "political struggle" in RVN to an "armed struggle."

May 1959 North Vietnam begins major improvements on the Ho Chi Minh Trail and sends troops to RVN.

October 1959 Communist Party and Vietminh outlawed by RVN.

December 20, 1960 NLF is formed.

May 5, 1961 US announces that support troops will be deployed to RVN.

January 1, 1962 PRP established in RVN.

February 6, 1962 Military Assistance Command, Vietnam (MACV) formed to control US armed forces in RVN.

January 2, 1963 ARVN troops defeated by VC at Ap Bac, their first major success.

April 17, 1963 RVN institutes Chieu Hoi (Open Arms) Program, providing amnesty to VC.

August 2–4, 1964 US destroyers attacked by North Vietnamese torpedo boats in the Gulf of Tonkin.

August 7, 1964 US Congress passes Gulf of Tonkin Resolution to counter North Vietnamese aggression.

February 7, 1965 VC attacks US installations in Pleiku. US authorizes air attacks on North Vietnam, commencing February 24.

March 8, 1965 First US Marine ground combat troops arrive in RVN.

April 6, 1965 US ground troops authorized to conduct offensive operations; this was not announced publicly until June 8.

May 7, 1965 First US Army conventional ground combat troops arrive in RVN.

September 2, 1965 First of seven PLA divisions organized.

October 25, 1966 US offers to withdraw all troops six months after North Vietnam withdraws from RVN.

December 1967 Antiwar protests occur more frequently and gain strength in US.

January 30, 1968 VC and NVA initiate Tet Offensive, which ends on February 26 with heavy VC/NVA losses.

March 31, 1968 US announces de-escalation of its war effort and halts bombing of North Vietnam.

May 12, 1968 Peace talks begin in Paris.

September 1968 "Mini Tet" Offensive launched by remaining VC and is defeated.

June 8, 1969 US initiates "Vietnamization Program" to completely turn the war effort over to RVN.

June 8, 1969 PRG formed in RVN by NLF.

September 2, 1969 Ho Chi Minh dies.

April 29, 1970 Offensive operations into Cambodia to neutralize NVA/VC sanctuaries.

August 18, 1971 Last Australian and New Zealand troops withdraw.

March 30, 1972 NVA Easter Offensive (Nguyen Hue Campaign) commences, lasting most of the year.

January 15, 1973 US announces halt to all offensive ground action.

January 27, 1973 Ceasefire agreement is signed in Paris.

March 29, 1973 Last US troops withdraw.

April 29, 1975 US Embassy, Saigon, evacuated.

April 30, 1975 Saigon falls to NVA.

Mid-May 1975 Northern government officially makes it clear the NLF and PRG have no part in the new Vietnam.

July 2, 1976 North and South Vietnam officially unified.

ORGANIZATION

PLA forces

The organization of PLA units is complex and confusing. This is partly due to the difficulty in translating Vietnamese organizational terms into English. The term *doan*, for example, means "group" and *don* "unit," but these could identify units of different sizes by adding a prefix. To make matters worse, the ARVN, NVA, and PLA often gave different meanings to different organizational terms. What meant a "section" to one was a "regiment" to another. There were also variations in organization between areas – the NLF and PLA purposely made the organization complex to confuse enemy intelligence. Furthermore, the categories of units recognized by Free World forces differed. The ARVN recognized five categories of units (regimental cadres, battalions, mobile companies, local companies, and local platoons) and the United States acknowledged only four (regiments, battalions, local companies, and local platoons) and called two by several different titles. Generally one hears only of Local Forces and Main Forces, but it was undeniably more complex.

PLA units were controlled by different echelons of the NLF. The NLF Central Committee, with the PLA High Command, controlled Main Force regiments and battalions. The Main Force (Bo Doi Chu Luc), or "hard hats" were full-time soldiers organized into battalions (*tieu doan*), regiments (*trung doan*), and, from late 1965, divisions (*su doan*). They were well armed and structured along conventional light infantry lines. They were relatively well educated (could read and write), were in good physical condition, and were well trained and indoctrinated. The units, though, were increasingly filled with NVA troops, and the divisions and many regiments fell under NVA control. Main Forces were classed as *thoat ly*, to be "cut off," meaning they had no ties, i.e. they were mobile. Lower-echelon forces and guerrillas supported them. Many Main Force fighters volunteered, or were encouraged by political officers and cadre to work in fields to support the unit, following a Main Force motto, "*Tu luc canh sinh*" – "We support ourselves."

The next echelon was under the control of provincial central committees, which controlled Regional Forces (Bo Doi Dia Phuong), sometimes called "Territorial Forces" or "Mobile Forces." These too were considered Main Forces operating in battalions and companies. The battalions could be independent (*tieu doan co dong*) or concentrated (*tieu doan tap trung*). The concentrated battalions, also called mobile battalions, were usually assigned to regiments, with which they might not be physically located except when concentrated for operations.

Battalion and regimental operations became increasingly common from 1965 as the nature of the armed struggle changed. Battalions had 250–500 men, although there were usually fewer troops rather than more. Ideally a regiment was 2,000 men, and a battalion numbered 600. A battalion usually had three companies, but two companies were common. There were also independent Regional Force companies (*dai doi doc lap*) operating under district control. These were gray-area entities as they were manned by more highly indoctrinated and motivated Guerrilla Popular Army (GPA) part-timers, but performed special missions, similarly to the Regional Forces. They conducted armed propaganda meetings in non-NLF-controlled villages and attacked strategic hamlets and government officials.

There was no standard company organization; they might have from 20–100+ men, with 40–50 being common. A 20–40-man company might be organized like a platoon with 2–4 squads. A larger company might have 2–4 platoons. Crew-served weapons were few and might be part of platoons or in separate platoons. There were companies with two or more small-weapons platoons, each with a mortar, machine gun, and perhaps a recoilless rifle.

The cadre

The cadre (*luc luong nong cot* or simply "can bo") was somewhat mysterious to Free World forces, but a major factor in the life of the VC. The term referred to several categories of personnel. Recruiting cadres from the district were usually responsible for convincing young men and women to join the PLA. Political and administrative cadres were assigned at all levels – village, district, provincial, etc. – and they operated the central committees and the many NLF and PRP associations and organizations. They were different from military cadres. Military cadres were in the positions of assistant squad leader upwards, the equivalent of NCOs and officers. In reality the military cadre was simply those in leadership positions. However, to be selected and promoted one had to demonstrate

PLA Divisions

1 PLA Division	Dec 10, 1965
2 PLA Division	Oct 20, 1965
3 PLA Division	Sept 2, 1965
5 PLA Division	Oct 23, 1965
7 PLA Division	Jun 13, 1966
9 PLA Division	Sep 2, 1965
10 PLA Division	Sep 20, 1972

The divisions were activated out of sequence and gaps left in the numbering to confuse intelligence efforts and make the PLA appear to be a larger force than it actually was. Free World forces reported these as "VC divisions." There were also NVA divisions bearing some of the same numbers. Frequently changed codenames and numbers were assigned to units of all types.
(Courtesy of Alberto Seto)

military proficiency, leadership, motivational skills, and bravery under fire. The individual also required combat experience, at least a degree of literacy, and had to display virtue. This latter trait meant the soldier had to be moral and honorable. Unit political officers were considered cadre selected for their education, dedication, and motivation. Training cadre were specialist military instructors who were also politically prepared to motivate their trainees. Cadre were required to be members of the NLF or PRP. Socio-economic background was also a factor. If the individual came from a family of landowners, intellectuals, or even had "too much" education, he might be denied party membership and progression to cadre status. Improper virtue, lack of motivation, weakness in combat, and other flaws could cause someone to lose his cadre status.

Guerrilla Popular Army

At district level were found the Guerrilla Popular Army (Dan Quan du Kich, or GPA) units, the Local Forces. *Dan Quan* means "civilian troops" and *du Kich*, means "strike and run," which is used in the same context as "guerrilla." These were the militia, the village self-defense forces (*Luc Luong Nhan Dan tu ve*), the "farmer by day, guerrilla by night" grass roots VC. Villagers regarded them as local civilians rather than outsider soldiers, an important distinction to the peasant. The GPA was not a single organization or unified command like the PLA. It was a category of local units responsible to the district central committee and not part of the PLA, although they could operate under Main Force unit control when necessary.

Village guerrillas (*du Kich xa*) were inexperienced youths, older men and physically unfit men charged with static village defense, purely as a psychological presence. The combat guerrillas (*du Kich chien dau*) were fit young men given a degree of training. They conducted more active operations around villages, patrolling, planting booby traps, and making minor harassment actions against local government units. They collected intelligence and it was their job to be familiar with the area. They also supported Provincial and Main Forces, serving as guides, providing local information, warning them of government-patrolled areas, finding bivouac areas, and arranging the purchase of food. As the combat guerrillas gained experience, members would be selected for reassignment to progressively higher-echelon forces.

Villages comprised two or more small hamlets spread over a small area. The guerrillas were organized into cells or squads in each hamlet, which together would give the village a 3–4-squad platoon, in theory.

Guerrilla units had another responsibility, food production. They were to stockpile food for higher-echelon independent units and to support themselves. They were not supposed to rely on external support, thereby not placing a burden on the system. They were to be self-sufficient in work and pay their own way. Of course, this system led to the unsanctioned collection of "war taxes," the guerrilla units strongly encouraging donations from villagers.

The PLA and NLF organization was often depicted as a simplistic, orderly structure with a platoon in a village, a company in a district, a battalion in a province, and a regiment in an inter-zone area. The village platoons were not components of district companies and those companies were not part of the provincial battalion; they were separate units.

RECRUITMENT

The reasons a man or woman joined the VC were as varied and complex as the individuals themselves. However, the basic reasons can be broken down into several categories. The most common was simply disillusionment with the Saigon government and an acceptance of the constant barrage of NLF propaganda. Often the only contact villagers had with the government was through heavy-handed tax collectors and ARVN soldiers. Saigon was a place they had only heard of. The peasant's loyalties were to his or her family and village. They wished only to farm and raise their families. Beyond that, district, province, and national government had no meaning.

The frequency of government visits was in direct relation to the village's distance from provincial and district headquarters. Tax collectors arrived escorted by soldiers. With them came Rural Development Cadre (RDC; previously Revolutionary Development Cadre, but this was changed due to the NLF's concept of waging "revolutionary warfare"), 59-person teams with their own security. These were idealistic young men and women, usually from the cities or sometimes recruited locally. They would spend six months at a village to establish a government presence, indoctrinate the people with lectures, commence school and public-health projects, eliminate any NLF cadre, and expel corrupt village leadership. However, the concept of public service to help others was alien to the Vietnamese. The RDC had their

VC suspects are guarded by marines on a firebase. In VC-infested areas, young men of military age and without South Vietnamese government identity cards were arrested and interrogated by the National Police.

own problems with corruption and ineptitude, but some of these projects proved successful; so successful that half their personnel were wiped out by the VC, demonstrating the threat to their cause.

After 1965, ARVN and US troops were to blame for many turning to the VC. Government troops came from other parts of the country and bore no empathy for locals. They and US soldiers searched villages, arrested VC suspects – often innocent – and even burned homes, earning the remote government no friends. Americans were often seen as invaders with strange ways. It was difficult for the rural Vietnamese to see them as protectors, even when they came to provide medical and dental assistance, or to pass out seed, tools, and construction materials. Government Popular Force (PF) outposts located at larger villages compounded this hatred of government soldiers. The outpost troops were locally recruited from unemployed young men, and their image was one of lazy, disrespectful louts who hid in their little fortress at night when the VC entered the village in search of food and recruits. Other government militia such as the Regional and Popular Forces were little better. Collectively known as "Ruff/Puffs," the RF was a provincial militia and the PF a village defense militia known as the Civil Guard and Self-Defense Corps, respectively, prior to 1964.

Initially the VC recruited from among specially selected candidates, highly motivated 17–30-year-olds in good physical condition, promising them that service would be near their homes. They investigated recruits, asking questions of neighbors and village NLF-appointed cadres. Social class was a factor, as the VC was an organization for the people, the workers, and peasants. The sons of businessmen, government officials, intellectuals, and large land-owners were rejected. This changed in 1963 when some became convinced that they could redeem the sins of their relatives by serving the NLF.

Physical and health condition standards were also lowered around this time and the maximum age was raised to 40. In 1964 recruiters were directed to enact a levy on 18–35-year-olds. Recruits were forced to join in order to meet the provincial quotas and there were no more promises of service near home; this turned away many potential recruits. By 1964 recruiters often met only a third of their quotas. The situation worsened as the VC suffered greater losses due to increased American presence and a more aggressive ARVN. In 1967 some 60–70 percent of the VC was drafted. After the 1968 Tet Offensive VC recruits all but dried up.

The NLF recruiting cadre was secretive regarding recruits and they would single out likely individuals and gradually convince them to join. This would be done through repeated visits over weeks and even months. Several arguments were used. One of the strongest was that they would be drafted anyway by the ARVN when they turned 18. In this regard the VC was in direct competition for manpower with their enemy, as they both drafted from the same pool. They were asked if they were willing to fight and die for a weak, unseen American puppet government. At least with the VC they might stay near home. The ARVN policy was to send recruits to distant parts of the country so they would be less tempted to desert or have family ties with local VC.

Another argument was whether they wanted to sit at home with their families while others sacrificed everything to fight for them and their freedom from imperialism. Many men had relatives and friends already serving in the VC. They too might pay a visit to shame them into joining. Village girls sympathetic to the cause would ask when they would join. They were told they needed to make a decision; they could not sit on the fence or hide behind their mothers. Some were promised a better education and also training that would earn them respect and an improved living when the NLF took over. If they were still reluctant, they might be told that they were either with the VC or against them. It was implied that their families might suffer if they made the wrong decision.

Some individuals were reluctant to join the VC as they had relatives in the ARVN or government, but they were told that the sins of their relatives would not be held against them and they could redeem their family by serving the cause. Even former ARVN soldiers and militiamen were recruited. If reliable they were valued for their training and experience. Still others joined because they believed it was glamorous, or for the adventure, to impress relatives and friends, or to leave behind dull village life. Some were promised government jobs as part of an NLF victory. The way to advancement, however, was not in the Local Forces, but the Main Force and this too was an inducement to volunteer for more distant and dangerous duty.

When levies were established most recruiters still attempted to persuade potential recruits, telling them volunteering would mean better assignments closer to home – they and their families would be viewed in a more favorable light. Little time was allowed for such tactics, however, and often the young men were gathered by a visiting NLF cadre escorted by VC and simply told they were leaving.

Moreover, there was the matter of VC atrocities, which many had witnessed. It was standard practice for the VC to enter a village, assemble the villagers, and parade out the government-appointed officials and any Self-Defense and RF/PF soldiers caught in their homes. Speeches were made extolling the NLF and the crimes against the people by the puppet government lackeys cowering before them. They were charged, judged, and condemned on the spot to be tortured and butchered before the villagers. The officials' families, women and children, often perished with them, being disemboweled or beheaded. Such tactics achieved several goals: they eliminated the tenuous government influence; taught the villagers that it was best not to support the government; demonstrated that the VC were in control and that the government and military were unable to protect them; and that when the VC asked for something, including their sons, resistance was futile. This was remembered when the cadres came to fill their levies. Even the relatives of murdered government officials were known to join the VC in an attempt to redeem themselves. It was not just about personal redemption, and survival, but the redemption of their family. The VC could be benevolent benefactors or savage terrorists.

Women were also recruited, although in limited numbers. In the eyes of the NLF, women were equal, at least in theory. The Local Forces made wide use of women in auxiliary tasks, but some were employed in the Main Forces. They served as nurses, radio operators, cadre members, cooks, intelligence operatives, administrators, porters, and laborers. Few were actual fighters, although they were seen taking part in guerrilla and Local Force patrols and were sometimes engaged in combat. It was a patriarchal culture, which nonetheless cultivated strong-willed women,

A posed photograph of three female VC armed with .30-cal. M1 carbines. They wear black uniforms with some khaki components and black and white scarves. While details are not clear, the woman to the left carries mostly homemade gear. (Keystone/Getty Images)

but they were encouraged to remain in the background. Aggressive and overly ambitious women were disapproved of and they were held to strict moral standards. Married and engaged women were not allowed to enlist. Indeed, the NLF's advancement of women did establish the seed for the Vietnamese women's movement. By 1967, though, female volunteers dropped drastically.

The VC also recruited among the minorities, but prejudices limited this: the Montagnards, Cambodians, and various ethnic Chinese group were largely shunned. Minorities were formed into a small number of units of common ethnicity. More often they were used as laborers, porters, and scouts and guides. They were not generally trusted.

Whether volunteering or drafted, recruits were often told that the would be gone only for a short time as they marched off into the night with a few meager possessions, accompanied by the cadre and their escorts.

TRAINING

The extent and quality of training received by the VC varied greatly. I depended on the type of unit, military situation in the area, training resources, and leadership. Basically, instruction was presented to small groups. Most of this was in the form of lectures and repetition. The degree of hands-on training depended on the availability of weapon and equipment. Tactical training, especially at the individual and small unit levels, did involve practical exercises. Chalkboards and terrain models were used to teach tactics and techniques. Antiaircraft training was conducted with wooden models of aircraft on poles held by a man running across a clearing as recruits dry-fired while trying to gauge the correct amount of lead. Cardboard silhouettes of helicopters were suspended on a pulley-rope between trees and pulled across while riflemen shot at them. Students were generally discouraged from asking questions and taking notes. The instruction would be repeated and they would be told everything they needed to know. If one asked too many questions or made notes he came under suspicion as a security risk, perhaps even a spy. There were instructors, though, who did encourage questions and gave careful instruction.

Most fighters first served in local units. Often they did simple jobs such as standing guard in the village and manning lookout posts to warn of government troops. They were often disappointed and bored of endless guard shifts. However, this experience provided an important period of scrutiny to check their reliability and they also received a good deal of political indoctrination. Once they were accepted by the unit, simple on-the-job training was provided and eventually the recruit would accompany local patrols.

Many would go on to Local, Regional, and Main Force units. This could denote progression or might be because a higher-level unit needed replacements after being weakened in battle. Units would be assigned levy quotas for replacements and they might gain their practical training in combat or through other forms of unit training. Depending on how well unit training programs were organized this could be quite effective. There were many variations between training programs and little standardization except for within provinces or the units themselves. Before assignment to a unit, recruits might undertake 5–8 days' training in basic skills such as marching, firing positions, individual movement, grenade throwing, bayonet-fighting, and at least two days of political indoctrination. This training was provided by a dozen training cadre members, and might be presented to groups of 30–70 men. Marksmanship training was limited owing to ammunition

Women were employed by the village guerrilla self-defense forces. While mainly used for auxiliary tasks, they were taught rudimentary combat skills. Here they are being instructed in the use of the .30-cal. M1 carbine. (Central Press/Hulton Archive/ Getty Images)

Discovered by Troop E, 2d Squadron, 11th Armored Cavalry Regiment southwest of Chu Lai, these VC sketches on the inside of a hootch (hut) were used in training to demonstrate how to engage American helicopters.

The Chinese-made Type 884 backpack radio made its appearance in the late 1960s. The man-packed radio was rugged, simple to operate, and reliable. It could transmit to a range of 7–10 miles (10–16km) by AM (voice) and over 100 miles (160km) by continuous wave (Morse code). It had a limited frequency range, making it easier to intercept. (William Howard Technical Intelligence Museum)

shortages or because firing would attract attention; generally dry-fire and aiming exercises were undertaken instead.

Once an individual was assigned to a battalion, up to a month' training was provided. Six or seven days of this would be politica indoctrination interspersed with individual and small-unit tactics including instruction in weapons, camouflage, fortifications, sanitation patrolling, movement techniques, discipline, and guard duty. Often thi training was of a good standard as it was generally provided by comba veterans who had practical experience and were keen to ensure that th men who would be fighting alongside them were thoroughly trained.

The recruit would finally be assigned to a company within th battalion, where the training continued. This involved more small-uni tactics, and ambush, assault, antihelicopter, and live-fire weapon training preceded by an hour of morning calisthenics. Some units woul move to secure areas, "liberated zones" clear of Free World forces, o even into Cambodia or Laos. There were mortar training bases insid Cambodia and practical exercises would be conducted by firing on Fre World bases inside Vietnam.

Specialty training courses were another means of improvin; effectiveness. Such courses were conducted by higher commands o military zones. The length of course varied greatly. Section, platoon, an company leader courses were three, five, and six months long respectively. Machine gunners, mortarmen, and recoilless rifle gunner undertook up to four months of training. Radio operators, who had t learn Morse code, and radio repairmen took six and 12-month courses

Such training was often provided by NVA cadremen. Classes wer divided into two groups with one group undertaking instruction whil the other moved supplies, provided guards, and conducted securit patrols. The next day the groups switched and the training was repeated Some training centers were long established and featured wooden barracks, kitchens, supply rooms, and other support facilities. Other training was conducted in remote unit base camps. In some cases training was given in an area surrounded by friendly villages and the students were quartered and fed by the villagers.

A major problem encountered by the VC was the poor level of literacy among peasants. The average education was 2½ years with 5–15 percent of peasants illiterate. Cultural instruction was provided in basic reading, writing, and math several hours a week.

Indoctrination

Political indoctrination was fundamental to the philosophy of the NLF. Ideally, half of the training time would be dedicated to indoctrination, although in practice the needs of combat training limited it to a quarter or less of the training time. Indoctrination was presented by trained NLF cadremen, unit leaders, or political officers.

Indoctrination encompassed orientation on rules and policies, leadership skills, unit traditions, communist doctrine, the evils of imperialism and capitalism, the misdeeds and corruption of the puppet government, treatment of civilians, and current events as seen through the eyes of the NLF. An important part of indoctrination and integration into the unit was self-criticism (*phe binh*) sessions. This was an alien concept to the Vietnamese, who kept personal feelings to themselves. Loss of face, being proven wrong, or being forced publicly to admit faults, mistakes, and omissions was something that proved extremely difficult for them to accept. Many never really did, but self-criticism was a cornerstone of the communist system and inherited from the Maoist Chinese communist philosophy. The idea was to learn from one's mistakes and correct them. The soldiers would also review lessons learned regarding morale, discipline, and motivation. This was the *kiem thao* session, which would be attended by all fighters, leaders, and cadre. Subordinates, however, did not criticize superiors, and non-NLF members could not comment on the actions of party members even if of lesser rank.

Political indoctrination within the VC was just as important as military training. Mandatory sessions were conducted daily by the unit's political cadre.

APPEARANCE

One of the major frustrations of American soldiers was that it was impossible to tell the difference between a peasant farmer and a guerrilla fighter. Guerrillas and Local Forces especially made every effort to blend in with the population. The VC was mostly ethnic Vietnamese and purposely and easily integrated themselves into communities. As mentioned previously, there were other ethnic groups represented in the VC, including Montagnards (mountain tribesmen), Cambodians (Khmers) born and raised in Vietnam, Nungs, Hmong and Hoa (the latter three being ethnic Chinese.) However, the ethnic Chinese were only found in small numbers and while employed by the VC they were not fully accepted owing to deep-seated Vietnamese prejudices.

The average Vietnamese male was 5ft 1in.–5ft 4in. (1.57–1.63m) tall, weighing 110–122lb (50–55kg). In comparison, the average American soldier was 5ft 8in. (1.73m) and carried another 20–30lb (9–14kg). North Vietnamese tended to be slightly taller than southerners and of lighter complexion. The VC kept their hair cut a little longish on the sides and tops to match the style of the farmers. In Main Forces, however, and even in some local units they bore what was known as an "NVA haircut," short on the sides and nape and longish on top. This haircut gave away many VC. Main Forces often looked leaner, harder and were in better condition than their Local Force counterparts.

VC Local Force personnel unpack Chinese antitank rifle grenades from their black metal packing tubes and insert detonators, readying them for action. To protect the munitions from dirt, the work is accomplished on rice straw mats. (Keystone/ Getty Images)

Local Forces

The "standard uniform" of guerrilla and Local Forces was that of the people: a simple collarless black shirt and trousers with few, if any, pockets. Often the cotton shirt was fastened by white or tan buttons. This was the traditional peasants' garb, the *bo do den* (black outfit), which Americans called "black pajamas" or "black P.J.s." A similar white outfit was also worn, the *bo do danh tu*. There was also a more formal high-necked white shirt called the *cu-nao*. Medium- to dark-blue outfits (*bo do xuan*) were also worn and the colors of the shirts and trousers might be mixed. Shorts were commonly worn, as were white undershirts. However, the VC tended to wear the black or dark-blue outfits more regularly.

The VC would wear any form of civilian clothing depending on their mission, including Western styles if reconnoitering Free World facilities or when acting as couriers. Footwear could be the many forms of sandals (*dep, xang dan*) including the wood shoes (*quoc*), and rubber shower shoes ("flip-flops"), which the Vietnamese called Japanese slippers (*dep nhat*). Durable Ho Chi Minh sandals, or what the VC called tire sandals (*dep vo xe*), with truck-tire soles and inner-tube straps, were common. Flat-soled canvas sneakers were also worn. The wide, conical rice straw hat (*non la*) was worn for both sun and rain protection.

Main Forces

Main Force units wore uniforms similar to the NVA troops. Regional Forces were also similarly dressed, but when in their home areas they would make every effort to blend in, as Local Forces did. By 1968 most Main Force units were filled largely with NVA and the few remaining VC were given the same equipment as them.

Dark-green uniforms were issued; these were made of lightweight cotton, the shirts might have one or two breast pockets, with or without flaps, and narrow collars. The green shades varied greatly and other colors were used, including dark blue (called "blue khaki" by Americans), olive drab, brown, and khaki (tan) shades. Black outfits were sometimes carried and changed into for blending with the population. It was not uncommon for different colors of shirts and trousers to be mixed. ARVN and even US uniform components were occasionally worn.

The most common headgear was the broad-brimmed jungle hat. These had a rounded crown, whereas ARVN and US-style "bonnie hats" were flat-topped, and were found in the same colors as uniforms. NVA light olive-green or tan cloth-covered fiber pith helmets were also common, hence Main Forces and NVA were sometimes called "hard hats" (*non coi*). Chinese and Soviet steel helmets were sometimes issued and known as *non sac*.

Long black and white checkered and striped scarves, as well as solid red scarves, were worn looped once around the neck as sweat cloths and towels. Khmer Rouge (Cambodian communist) red and white striped scarves saw some use. Other colors were used for friend-or-foe

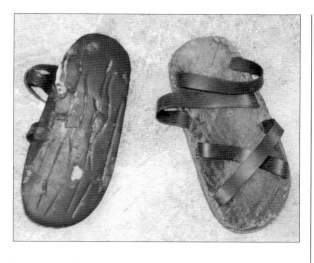

A pair of Ho Chi Minh sandals, or what the VC called tire sandals (*dep vo xe*). Their extremely worn automobile or truck-tire tread soles are barely visible. (Steve Sherman)

Main Force fighters assault through a forest, routing Free World forces. The VC are armed with AK-47s and RPDs. (Keystone/Hulton Archive/Getty Images)

recognition. A comparatively small cape of US four-color nylon parachute cloth was widely used for camouflage. It was square or rectangular with rounded corners. Upper corners were knotted on the chest and it was worn in such a manner as to cover the shoulders, upper arms, and the back to include the rucksack. When not needed for camouflage it was folded as a scarf around the neck.

Green canvas and black rubber boots were widely used, as were looted US- and Canadian-made Vietnamese boots. A pair of sandals was always carried for camp wear to rest the feet and as back-up footwear. The VC also donned sandals when wading streams, swamps, rice paddies, and monsoon-flooded areas.

The VC had no rank insignia; they used position titles instead (the NVA had collar rank insignia, but this was seldom worn in the South). A small metal badge was sometimes worn on the front of hats and fiber helmets. There were a few decorations awarded for valor and service. The individual fighters cared for their own clothing and equipment, making minor repairs. They were frequently encouraged to preserve their equipment, as replacement items were scarce.

WEAPONS AND EQUIPMENT

The VC used whatever weapons and equipment they could lay their hands on. Standardization was unheard of. The sources of weapons and equipment were as diverse as the gear itself. A great deal was shipped from the north overland on the Ho Chi Minh Trail (officially called the Duong Truong Son – Truong Son Road – named after the mountains it crossed) and down the coast by small ships and junks. Most armaments, equipment, and supplies came from China, with a large amount supplied by the USSR and Warsaw Pact states.

In the early days much of what was provided by China was obsolete and came from several sources. The Nationalist Chinese had used German, Czechoslovak, Belgian, French, Canadian, British, and Swiss weapons, and examples from all these nations showed up in Vietnam. A few of the weapons were license-produced in China prior to the communist takeover. A great deal of US equipment was also supplied by China, and was usually assumed to be from stocks captured in Korea. Most US equipment finding its way to Vietnam, however, had been provided to the Nationalists during World War II. Some weapons were copied from US arms captured in Korea, and the Chinese produced their own versions. The Chinese also held a great deal of Japanese equipment and this too was sent south. Essentially, Vietnam became a dumping ground for old equipment, for which China was grateful. The USSR also shipped a lot of World War II weapons, including captured German armaments. From 1967 large quantities of modern Soviet weapons began to arrive along with their Chinese counterparts (bearing type designations).

The French left large volumes of armaments behind in Vietnam and these too were shipped from the North, as well as captured from RVN troops who were using them prior to the deluge of American supplies. French weapons continued to turn up through the war, along with other old weapons provided by China. Intelligence analysts were often left scratching their heads as to how some weapons ended up in Vietnam.

Besides US weapons provided by the Chinese, American weapons were captured from RVN forces, which were entirely equipped by the United States and other Free World forces. Not all US weapons used by the VC were valiantly captured in combat. Some were stolen from arriving ships before they left port (usually with the help of opportunist dockworkers and truck drivers), were bribed or extorted from ARVN troops, or were simply stolen and sold by soldiers themselves. Some ARVN commanders even sold weapons and reported them lost in combat or beyond repair.

Thousands of Soviet and Chinese-built trucks carried tons of supplies down the Ho Chi Minh Trail winding through Laos and Cambodia. This was not a single trail, but a complex network of interconnected improved roads and trails maintained by thousands of support troops.

A wide variety of weapons from sometimes unusual sources were used by the VC. Here a German World War II 7.92mm MG34 machine gun is used as an antiaircraft weapon. Spare parts, belts, magazines, and ammunition were difficult to obtain for such weapons, complicating the VC supply system.

The lower the level the VC unit the more outdated were its weapons. However, owing to lucky captures and bartering with the NVA, even guerrilla units might field a few modern weapons. The VC fabricated a lot of homemade armaments, but this was usually in the form of grenades, mines, booby traps, and demolitions rather than firearms.

Unlike many Americans, most Vietnamese had absolutely no familiarity with firearms, or, for that matter, any experience with anything mechanical or electrical. This was especially true of peasants. When the fighter was issued his first weapon, he held in his hands a completely alien implement vastly more complex than the rice sickle and hoe he was familiar with. He would learn fast, however, through rote instruction and constant handling.

The wide variety of small arms are far too numerous to discuss here, but some of the most common will be examined from the guerrilla's perspective. There were certain desirable characteristics for guerrilla weapons. They needed to be lightweight and compact, not only for use in jungle fighting, fighting positions and tunnels, but to make them easier to conceal and transport covertly. Reliability and ruggedness were also required, not only for the obvious needs of combat, but because replacements and repair parts were scarce. Models of weapon with easily obtainable ammunition were essential. Some of the odd obsolescent weapons required scarce German or Czechoslovak ammunition, for example. US weapons were advantageous because ammunition could be obtained from government or US units, again, not always captured in combat, but bought from government troops, donated by sympathizers, pilfered, or recovered in the field; both government and US units were often careless.

A weapon on which many guerrilla and Local Forces cut their teeth was the Soviet 7.62mm Mosin-Nagant M1944 (Chinese Type 53) carbine called the "K44" or "red stock rifle" owing to its reddish-stained stock. When fitted with a Chinese grenade launcher it was an "AT44." Being short-barreled and lightweight at 8.9lb (4kg), it had an uncomfortable recoil for the physically smaller Vietnamese. This five-shot weapon

In the late 1950s and early 1960s, the VC were still reliant on homemade weapons such as these crude handguns. Some of these were as dangerous to the shooter as the target.

however, was rugged, reliable, compact, and had good penetration through bamboo and brush. It also had an integral folding spike bayonet. (This was little used and was useless as a utility knife, as opposed to a detachable bayonet.) The weapon was simple to operate, disassemble, and clean. For units that seldom engaged in a standup fight, it was almost an ideal weapon.

Two early and widely distributed submachine guns were the French 9mm MaT-49 and the North Vietnamese 7.62mm K50. The latter was a modified version of the Soviet PPSh-41 with a shortened barrel jacket to lighten it, and was fitted with an AK-47 pistol grip and the MaT-49's wire telescoping stock. MaT-49s were also rebarreled to 7.62mm as 9mm stocks dwindled. Both weapons were light, strong, and compact, although the 7.62mm weapons, firing a little pistol cartridge, had very poor penetration. Regardless, these and any other submachine guns were prized owing to their convenient dimensions and high rate of fire, which made them invaluable for close combat and ambushes.

US .30-cal. semi-auto M1 and selective-fire M2 carbines were widely issued to government troops, and large numbers fell into VC hands. The carbine was only 36in. (91.4cm) long and weighed 5lb 6oz (2.5kg). Its very light recoil made it popular, but its penetration through brush and its knockdown power were wanting – it used a small cartridge not much more effective than a pistol round. While reliable enough, its small parts were prone to breakage, and a unit usually had to have a few damaged carbines from which they could cannibalize parts. Both 15- and 30-round magazines were available.

Other obsolete US weapons from World War II used by the ARVN fell into VC hands, such as the .30-cal. Garand M1 semi-automatic rifle, .30-cal. M1918A2 Browning automatic rifle (BAR), and .45-cal. Thompson M1A1 and M3A1 ("grease gun") submachine guns. All were heavy and bulky for the Vietnamese and the BAR and Thompson were difficult to maintain. The 5.56mm M16A1 rifle and 40mm M79 grenade launcher were also highly valued weapons, obtained from both US and, from 1968 on, government troops – they added lightweight firepower to the VC's arsenal.

However, the semi- and full-automatic M16 "black rifle" did require meticulous cleaning and had poor penetration through brush. The M79 was a real prize because of the high-explosive firepower it delivered.

In late 1967 NVA forces had largely withdrawn to Cambodia and Laos and began to rearm with AK-47 assault rifles. Their Soviet 7.62mm SKS (Chinese Type 56) carbines were turned over to VC Main Forces. The SKS was a relatively short weapon (40 1/6 in./102cm), fairly light (8.8lb/4kg) rugged, easy to maintain, semi-automatic with a ten-round magazine, and had light recoil. It was fitted with a folding bayonet. By the Tet Offensive in 1968 the NVA were entirely armed with the Soviet 7.62mm AK-47s (Type 56). Thus, it was not long before AKs began appearing in VC Main Force hands. What was to become the most widely distributed assault rifle in the world was an ideal weapon for the VC/NVA. It was comparatively

small for the firepower it produced, but it was heavy at 9lb 6oz (4.3kg), to which its robust 30-round magazine added 1lb 3oz (0.6kg). However, it was incredibly reliable and put a tremendous amount of automatic firepower into the hands of the individual fighter. Alongside the AK-47 came the arrival of the RPD (Type 56) light machine gun. At 15lb 6oz (7kg) it was four pounds lighter than the BAR, shorter, and was fed by a 100-round belt in a drum magazine rather than a 20-round magazine. It was not designed for long-range or sustained fire, but it was a close assault weapon ideal for guerrillas.

With such a wide variety of weapons in use and mixed within units, each fighter had to be familiar with ammunition. Four types of 7.62mm were in use, three of Soviet origin and the 7.62mm NATO. Contrary to myth none of the Soviet rounds were interchangeable with the 7.62mm NATO. The rimmed 7.62x54mm was used in bolt-action rifles, carbines, and heavy machine guns. The short 7.62x39mm round was used in the SKS, AK, and RPD. While it was a small cartridge, it was effective at the close-combat ranges it was intended for and its steel-cored bullet had good penetration. Another Soviet round was the 7.62x25mm pistol cartridge used in submachine guns. The 7.62x51mm NATO was used in M14 rifles and

A Main Force fighter activates a hand grenade's friction igniter. These men are armed with Chinese Type 56 (AK-47) assault rifles with folding spike bayonets. (Three Lions/Hulton Archive/Getty Images)

M60 machine guns. Two US .30-cal. rounds were used, a short round for the carbines and the much larger .30-06 for M1 rifles, BARs, and machine guns.

Pistols were of little use and were mainly seen as a sign of office for commanders and were sometimes used as assassination weapons. The little 7.62mm Tokarev TT-33 (Type 51) was common, as was the 9mm Makarov PM (Type 59), French 7.65mm M1935A, and US .45-cal. Colt M1911A1. All had eight-round magazines, except the Colt with seven rounds.

An important weapon was the RPG-2 (Type 56) antitank projector, commonly called the "rocket propelled grenade." This compact weapon was shoulder-fired, lightweight, and capable of knocking out most tanks, and could penetrate several feet of sandbags. It was so simple to operate that any fighter familiar with a rifle could be trained in an hour to fire it. The 40mm tube was loaded with an over-caliber 85mm shaped-charge projectile. In early 1968 a much improved, longer-ranged, more accurate and lethal RPG-7 (Type 67) made its appearance. The projectiles for the two weapons were entirely different. North Vietnamese-made versions were known as the B40 and B41 respectively, the "B" meaning *Badoka* – bazooka.

Hand grenades were widely used, and included US, Russian, and Chinese models, and many crude homemade types. Mines from these countries were also used.

Because mobility was essential to VC units, crew-served weapons were, by necessity, light. Artillery units were armed with mortars and recoilless rifles, and antiaircraft units with Soviet 12.7mm DShKM38/46 (Type 54) and US .50-cal. M2 machine guns. (While the 12.7mm was called ".51-cal.," the ammunition was not interchangeable with the US M2 as rumored.) Soviet 7.62mm rifle-caliber machine guns included the DPM (Type 53), RP-46 (Type 58), SG-43 (Type 53), and SGM (Type 57) as well as US .30-cal. M1919A4/A6s and 7.62mm M60s.

Mortars were relatively lightweight, indirect-fire weapons capable of inflicting a great deal of damage on fixed installations and exposed troops. Their ammunition was heavy, though, and required significant manpower to move. Mortars (*sung coi*) in common use included:

US 60mm M2 & M19
French 60mm M1935
Chinese 60mm Types 31 & 63*
US 81mm M1, M29, & M29A1
French 81mm M1931
Soviet 82mm PM37 (Type 53)†
Soviet 120mm HM43 (Type 55)
* While often called "61mm," they were
  60mm and their ammunition could be
  fired in US mortars.
† US 81mm ammunition could be fired, but
  Soviet/Chinese rounds could not be fired
  in US mortars.

Recoilless rifles or *Dai-bac Khong Ziat* (DKZ) were heavy, but could be man-packed cross-country. Their direct fire was useful for attacking bunkers, buildings, and vehicles. Other than the Soviet 73mm and 82mm versions, they were not too effective against armored vehicles. Types included:

US 57mm M18A1 recoilless rifle
Chinese 57mm Type 36
  recoilless rifle*
Soviet 73mm SPG-9 recoilless
  gun
US 75mm M20 recoilless rifle
Chinese 75mm Types 52 & 56
  recoilless rifles†
Soviet 82mm B-10 recoilless gun
* The Type 36 was a copy of the M18A1.
† The Types 52 & 56 were copies of the
M20.

The equipment carried by VC fighters was sparse. They traveled as light as possible and items that Western troops considered essential were often unnecessary luxuries to the VC. Guerrillas were seldom out for more than a night. If they were required on longer-duration missions they would make do with only the most essential items, receiving food and shelter from villagers. Regional and Main Forces carried basic equipment, but this too was spartan. Five days' worth of rations was the maximum amount carried.

Guerrillas usually carried what they needed in their pockets, with possibly some belt gear or a small haversack. It was imperative that they appeared little different from peasants and were able to discard military items quickly. For this reason they seldom carried valuable gear unless absolutely needed, which led to the American joke that a three-man VC cell comprised one man carrying an M1 carbine, one the magazine, and one a grenade.

Individual equipment may have been of Chinese, North Vietnamese, Soviet, Warsaw Pact, French, or American origin, often mixed together with homemade items. VC troops were sometimes seen with complete sets of US web gear. One VC squad engaged by the author's company was found with a few US web gear items, Coca Cola bottles and thermos jugs for water, school book satchels, small backpack wicker baskets, and 3ft 3-in.(1m) squares of green plastic folded into packets to hold rations and slung on the back with cords.

Regional and Main Forces also made use of homemade and captured gear, but later in the war they acquired much Chinese and NVA equipment. The gear was low cost and did not hold up well to rough treatment and the climate. Green shades predominated, but olive drab, brown, and tan gear were common.

The common green web belt was more like a trouser belt and was intended to carry only limited equipment. It usually had a two-piece interlocking steel buckle with a five-point star. Most gear was carried by shoulder straps rather than on the belt. Magazine pouches for AK-47s,

K50s, and other weapons usually had belt loops, but also shoulder straps, as did two- and four-pocket grenade pouches. The three-pocket AK-47 magazine chest pouch virtually became a symbol of the VC/NVA. The chest pouch even provided a minor degree of protection from bullets and fragments. Similar ten-pocket pouches, worn around the lower belly or waist, were available for the SKS.

Chinese- and North Vietnamese-made olive drab or green-painted aluminum canteens were in wide use, and were also fitted with belt loops and/or a shoulder strap. Mess gear was minimal, often a small tin pan or metal rice bowl, usually enameled, plus chopsticks, a spoon, and perhaps a tin cup. Military-style mess kits saw some use. Rice was carried in small plastic bags or fabric rice tubes worn horseshoe fashion over the shoulders.

This crude trip-wire activated crossbow will launch a char-hardened bamboo bolt down a trail. Such devices were actually little used and of limited effectiveness. Left for even a short time in the rain and heat they quickly deteriorated and became non-operational. (Keystone/Hulton Archive/ Getty Images)

The VC were industrious and ingenious. Their logistics support was minimal and they made their own repairs to damaged equipment. Here Chinese 57mm Type 36 and US 75mm M20 recoilless rifles are refurbished in a jungle workshop. Along with mortars, the recoilless rifles, or DKZs, were considered the VC's artillery.

Small canvas rucksacks were of North Vietnamese and Chinese origin. They had two or three pockets on the outside. Captured US rucksacks of different designs were also used. Locally made rucksacks and ammunition pouches copied North Vietnamese and Chinese designs, but were cruder and flimsier than the originals and were sometimes made of non-military colored fabric.

A canvas or nylon hammock was the normal sleeping accommodation. Sleeping on the ground was unhealthy owing to insects, snakes, leeches, rats, and damp earth. However, circumstances sometimes dictated that the fighters had no choice. If this was the case then they would pile leaves to make a bed and lie on a plastic sheet. Plastic sheets were multi-purpose items. They could be of any color, but were usually some shade of green; although blue and semi-clear were common. A crepe-paper-like textured light-green plastic was widely used. Besides being employed as a ground cloth they were also often pitched as fly tents over hammocks with cords tied to the corners and a lengthwise supporting ridge line. They were also worn as rain capes by draping a sheet over the shoulders and knotting the upper corners on the chest. Another use was to pitch the sheet as a low lean-to and cover it with vegetation for concealment from aircraft when a unit rested or awaited movement orders. Mosquito nets were essential in the wet season, but not always available. In the northern mountains blankets were used in the cool temperatures. Light jackets and sweaters were also necessary.

Chinese, Soviet, French, and US entrenching tools were used. If some form of belt carrier was not available they were carried horizontally under the rucksack flap. Rice sickles, knives, and short machetes were also used to cut camouflage and clear vegetation. Regular-sized shovels, pick-axes, and hoes were used for digging bunkers and fighting positions. Short-handled shovels, picks, hoes, and scrapers were used for tunneling, and wicker baskets were applied to haul out the earth.

Rucksack contents included rations, ammunition, grenades, utility knife, and spare clothing. A spare set of underwear and socks might also be carried. Personal items included a toothbrush (often a chewed wood

28

A collection of weapons and munitions captured from the VC by government troops. It includes French-made 9mm MaT-49 submachine guns, locally made stick hand grenades, and demolition charges. These appear to be three 14oz (400g) TNT blocks bound together by bamboo strips.

stick substituted), soap, comb, and towel, all in a plastic or cloth bag. A pair of sandals was carried for camp wear. If a fiber helmet was issued it was carried strapped to the rucksack, and a hat would be worn. Field dressings and bandages were carried in the rucksack, but placed in a pocket during combat. Journals, letters, family photographs, and a little red booklet, *A Short Biography of Ho Chi Minh*, would be carried wrapped in plastic.

A Main Force unit headquarters with its cadre, security personnel, and radio operators. Note the US AN/PRC-25 radios on the left front row. This demonstrates that even in Main Force units there was little uniformity.

Unit communications equipment was sparse and usually found at battalion and higher levels. FM voice radios were mostly of Chinese manufacture such as the Types 63, 139A, 883, and 884, as were Type 65 field telephones. These radios were relatively lightweight, backpack models with limited range. The VC also built homemade radios. These were AM transceivers housed in .50-cal. ammunition cans. They also used US backpack AN/PRC-25 and -77 radios.

CONDITIONS OF SERVICE

The experiences of the VC, as with any soldier, were varied and vastly differed according to units, areas, and timeframes.

Assigned to a guerrilla unit, a young, physically fit fighter would be a "combat guerrilla" rather than a "village guerrilla" fit only for static defense. The latter were kept busy with non-combat tasks, such as: collecting food, cooking duty, political indoctrination and military training sessions, and making the rounds talking to and inspiring civilians. They sometimes helped farmers with their chores to ally themselves with the people and gain support.

Guard duty was frequent. The guards had to be ever vigilant of enemy incursions. Even at night, when the enemy never came, they remained watchful. Guards were posted around the village's outlying hamlets and watched roads and trails. They might also be posted to watch distant large clearings and open fields to warn of the arrival of

VC attacks on Free World installations were characterized by detailed lengthy planning and preparations. Here a model of a government Popular Force platoon outpost is used to brief all personnel. Even the adjacent village's houses are represented. The VC unit will then conduct repeated rehearsals prior to executing the lightning-fast attack.

helicopters. Often young boys, wishing to become fighters, were employed in this way. More distant outposts were manned and the warning of an enemy's approach would be sounded with rifle shots, bamboo gongs, whistles, or horns. The VC learned where the many concealed dugouts and small tunnels were in which to hide rather than fight a superior force.

The new guerrilla would be integrated into his cell. The three-man cell was the basic element and foundation of VC unit structure, and as originally conceived the "secret guerrilla cell" (*du Kich bi mat*) was the core of guerrilla organization. The three cell members were known only to themselves. They would not know the members of other cells and only the cell leader would know the squad leader and so on up the chain-of-command. This worked for an underground organization, but this degree of secretiveness was impossible when subunits were required to operate as a single tactical unit. However, the cell always remained part of the unit structure. The cell worked, messed, quartered, and fought together. They were a miniature collective, a family, and were responsible for one another's actions. They provided moral support, reminded one another of their duties when they became lax, and criticized one another during self-criticism sessions. As an example, a company guard roster would not be composed of individuals drawn from within the unit on a rotating basis. A cell would be assigned a guard post and be responsible for manning that post through the night. Three cells made up a standard squad with the squad leader doubling as a cell leader. Squads could consist of 2–4 cells. Heavy weapons crews also functioned as a cell or might be organized as two or even three cells in larger crews.

The VC lived in the hamlets, sometimes sharing a home with villagers who fed them. At other times they lived in an unused house or one they built themselves. Food was also purchased locally. VC dressed as civilians and would shop in local markets, mingling with their enemies. They also purchased items off the lively black market, not just food and comfort items, but items of military value.

Patrols were conducted during the day, hiking between the hamlets and even making contact with the guerrillas of other villages. A cell or a squad would make these rounds as much to demonstrate their presence to the civilians they were defending as for security. This maneuver could be dangerous as it was the most likely time to make contact with an enemy patrol.

Often there was a government outpost manned by Popular Forces outside a larger village. The occupants seldom patrolled outside the village. Most were lazy and afraid to venture out. Surveillance was maintained on this platoon-size unit. The district central committee was very interested in its activities and the numbers and types of weapons it had. The little government outpost served as a training objective for the new guerrillas.

One of the first combat missions a guerrilla might participate in would be to serve as a "shouter." A District, Regional, or Main Force unit would attack a government outpost. Guerrillas would be sited around the outpost while the attacking unit moved into its assault position. The guerrillas would create a din, shouting, blowing whistles, banging gongs, and hitting sticks on trees. This resulted in panicked calls for reinforcement as the assault troops attacked. Consequently, subsequent media and military reports indicated that a battalion or more had attacked an outpost when only 50–70 fighters had been involved. Even if the attack failed the exaggerated reports gave the appearance of large VC units operating throughout the countryside.

Such an action would probably have been frightening for the new fighters initially, due to the great deal of noise and the tracers streaking overhead. However, once the firing had died down to occasional bursts the VC would often amuse themselves by exchanging shouted insults with the puppet defenders. Rarely would there be any real effort to penetrate the barbed wire around the outpost, and generally before it became light the guerrillas would fall back to their rally point. Sometimes these seemingly "sham" actions would turn out to be a distraction for a Main Force operation, as a Main Force unit would lie in wait to ambush a government convoy sent to rescue the seemingly beleaguered outpost. Such episodes allowed the new fighters to feel proud that they had contributed to the destruction of the puppet unit without having to engage in full combat.

After a few often boring months, young guerrillas deemed the most morally and politically motivated and militarily proficient were selected for transfer to District or Regional units. Assigned to a Regional Force the battalion proved to be a more military organization. It occupied a base camp in a remote area. The new arrivals learned that there were other camps scattered through the province that they could move to if this one was discovered. They might stay at a camp for a couple of weeks or just a few days. The camps were within a night's march of each other. The new soldiers also learned that there were secret caches of rice, ammunition and medical supplies hidden in the jungle. Only selected cadre knew where they were.

The results of a VC attack on a Popular Force outpost. A dead Regional Force soldier lies in the entrance of a mortar-blasted bunker.

Training and indoctrination intensified and the sessions alternated with guard duties, patrols, working on bunkers and quarters, hauling supplies, etc. The base camp was generally on a low, jungle-covered hill. It was irregular in shape and not on what would be thought of as militarily important terrain. It was distant from roads, trails and villages. There was a stream within a few hundred yards. Two- and three-man bunkers were sited around its perimeter and bomb shelters were scattered about. There were dugouts for command posts and cadre, and bamboo and thatch huts used for classes, eating, and sleeping. Bamboo sleeping platforms were built at some camps. Other VC simply hung hammocks with rain sheet covers. Some camps were laid out with the companies situated up to a kilometer apart. (See Osprey Fortress 48: *Viet Cong and NVA Tunnels and Fortifications of the Vietnam War.*)

Much time was spent patrolling the area. This activity also served as a means of additional training. It was a break in camp routine, with its many work details, and patrols would visit abandoned villages to forage in their overgrown

Training and indoctrination

A

Village Defense and Local Forces

B

Jungle grenade factory

c

Ambush

1

3

6a

2

5a

6

8

5

10

9

4

7

11

12

Firefight

Sappers

G

gardens and orchards for fruit and vegetables. Contrary to popular perception, the jungles were not sown with booby traps. These were found only around base camps and their approaches, around defended villages, and planted on enemy patrol routes around Free World bases. The new fighters were shown where booby traps were laid and the marking signs.

Meals were simple and somewhat monotonous. Cooked rice (*com*) was the basic staple eaten in all meals. The primary source of protein was *nuoc mam*, a pungent spiced fish sauce made by packing layers of anchovies and salt in barrels and fermenting it for months. It was as essential and popular as rice. Meat, mostly pork (*thit lon*), chicken (*ga*), and (if near rivers or the sea) fish (*ca*), was considered a side dish rather than the main course. A dipping sauce (*nuoc cham*) was the principal side dish condiment made from *nuoc mam* with lime juice, red peppers, and other spices. Most side dishes were dipped in this and then wrapped in edible rice paper or lettuce. Vegetables, especially cucumbers, were popular, but were in short supply. Wheat, rice, and mung bean noodles (*bun*) were another side dish and would be served alongside various soups (*pho*), especially bean. Most Vietnamese foods are heavily flavored with a wide variety of spices. Hot tea (*tra*) and an occasional beer (*bia hoi*) were the principal drinks. A frequent complaint was that the rice was either undercooked or burnt. It was difficult to cook it in large amounts and at the same time reduce the fire smoke. Cells and squads preferred to cook their own in small portions.

Personal conduct was held to a high standard by the cadre. Civilians were to be treated with respect, especially women. Women in the PLA were not to be fraternized with, although inevitably this occurred. However, there were official prostitutes who served the cause, known as "joy girls." They charged a minimal fee, but their visits to units were rare occasions. Alcohol consumption was discouraged and kept to a minimum. Some fighters would manage to buy rice wine and beer from villagers though. Most fighters smoked, but it was difficult and costly to buy cigarettes. There was a black market for the favored American brands, with the popular menthols being the most costly. Most fighters rolled their own with pungent country tobacco.

Membership of the PLA was paid, but guerrillas received next to nothing, except for a small allowance. Interrogation reports show that there was no standard pay scale, with payment varying widely between units and periods. Payment was sporadic and the amount disbursed varied with each allotment. It might be the equivalent of a few US dollars or be up to 20–30 dollars, but the larger amounts were rare. In some areas low ranks received more than leaders did in others.

Decorations were awarded for valor and service, but as with pay this was unusual. Liberation War Exploit Order, Soldier of Liberation Order, Soldier of Liberation Decoration, and Valiant Soldier Assault Decoration are examples. Awards were usually provided in three classes depending on the degree of valor. The Brass Fortress Order was presented both to individuals and units. In 1977 it was blanket-awarded to all units and individuals who had not yet been decorated for the 1975 victory. Medals were suspended on blue and red ribbons, the NLF colors.

VC recruits were taught about their different enemies. ARVN soldiers were forcibly drafted and few had their hearts in the struggle. It was

Fighters, armed with Type 56 (SKS) carbines, assault Free World forces through burning brush. Vegetation was often set alight by flares, smoke grenades, tracers, etc. The VC would sometimes intentionally set brush afire to screen their movements. (Three Lions/Hulton Archive/Getty Images)

different for the Vietnamese paratroopers, rangers, and marines. The regular troops were puppets, whereas the elite units were motivated and dangerous fighters. The Regional and Popular Forces were rabble, of little concern. The Civilian Irregular Defense Group (CIDG) mercenaries were led by the American Special Forces. They were hated not only because they were mercenaries, but also because most of them were Cambodians and Montagnards. The Americans were especially despised. They were considered to be invaders from the other side of the world. This was a war of their making and they had no business here. They told the puppet Saigon government what to do and lavished it with arms and money to keep the war going. Seldom would the VC take prisoners from the ARVN elite units and the CIDG. They sometimes spared the regular ARVNs and a few were even turned after re-education. If not they were used for labor in the rear bases. To kill an American was a great honor, a demonstration of combat skill and valor. However, the VC was under strong orders from the NLF to take American prisoners if at all possible.

Often VC troops would be alerted for a mission, thinking that they were about to be sent into combat, and instead a platoon was sent to sweep an area that an American unit had passed through. Americans were notorious for discarding what they believed was trash on the battlefield, but such items proved treasure to the VC: expended smoke grenades, safety levers and pins, LAW tubes, Claymore mine components, ammunition boxes and containers, grenade and projectile packing tubes, propellant containers, packing materials, pallets, sandbags, bandoleers, loading clips, machine-gun links, empty C-ration cans, mortar increments (propellant bags), artillery projectile booster charges (removed from fuse wells), expended "pop-up" flare tubes, expended time fuse igniters, field telephone wire, expended batteries, used field dressings, IV (intravenous) bottles, and other soiled medical items.

Local Forces and other units would also send salvage teams onto battlefields after the Free World forces had departed. The ARVN and other Free World forces were no better at litter discipline than US units, although there were always units performing better practices than others. Patrols trailing Free World units would recover whatever was left

behind at bivouac sites and even dig up trash and latrine pits. Abandoned fire support bases were also searched. These were a more dangerous proposition, though. Ambush patrols and snipers were often left behind along with booby traps, and occasionally a few artillery rounds were tossed in at irregular intervals for a few days after the base's closure. Higher headquarters often inspected closed out bases to ensure that nothing was left behind. Sometime CS (tear-gas powder) was spread over the bulldozed bases.

Literally everything left on the battlefield was of use to the VC. Expended smoke grenades, safety levers, and pins were remanufactured into casualty-producing grenades. Claymore firing devices and firing wires were reused for command-detonated mines. Ammunition cans had watertight gaskets and besides being reused for munitions, were used to hold human waste in tunnels and bunkers; the cans were later carried out, emptied, and reused. Projectile packing tubes made waterproof containers for supplies and were incorporated into booby traps, as were C-ration cans. The cans were also reworked into cooking utensils, stoves, and lamps. Mortar increments and artillery booster charges packed into containers made explosive booby traps. "Pop-up" flare tubes were made into pipe-bombs. Old fuse igniters used for demolition charges could be re-primed. Damaged sandbags and telephone wire were repaired. The author found when examining VC base camps that "commo wire" was a principal construction material for binding and guy lines, as well as for securing and repairing rucksacks and carrying bags. Wooden ammunition boxes and pallets provided timber for camp furniture, as well as hinges and latches plus solid storage boxes. "Dead" radio and flashlight batteries often retained sufficient juice to initiate an electric blasting cap in command-detonated mines and electrically activated booby traps. An "expended" battery's charge could be slightly increased by warming it next to a fire. The VC would tear discarded olive-green M16 rifle bandoleers into thin strips and tie them together to use as booby trap tripwires, which were difficult to detect when concealed among vegetation. Loading clips and machine-gun links were reused, as were discarded "worn out" uniform items. The VC even recycled surgical tubing, syringes, and IV needles

More elaborate arms factories were hidden in tunnels and caves. Here large metal lathes turn out weapons parts. The machines were stolen after arriving at seaports with the aid of opportunist dock workers, criminals, or sympathizers. (Keystone/Hulton Archive/Getty Images)

found on the battlefield. Bloody field dressings and gauze pads were washed and reused. They picked up the little discarded individual C-ration salt and sugar packets. A packet each of salt and sugar in a canteen of water helped revive a heat exhaustion casualty. Discarded leaking 2-quart bladder canteens were repaired and used for whole blood transfusions or home-brewed saline solutions. At one point the US stopped issuing bladder-type canteens as they were so widely used by the VC. Heavy-duty plastic 81mm mortar round containers with gasketed screw-on caps were packed with shaved ice from a town's little confectionery shop, in which bottled whole blood was packed, having been donated by rear service troops immediately prior to an operation.

BELIEF AND BELONGING

To understand the VC fighter some basic aspects of the Vietnamese culture need to be appreciated.

Confucianism

Vietnamese culture and society were strongly shaped by Confucianism, even among individuals practicing other religions or communism. The teachings of Confucius influence the position of the individual in society. The philosophy stresses benevolence, duty, propriety, conscience, and faithfulness (*nhon, nghia, le, tri, tin*) along with respect for age and seniority. It is a system of ethics and behavior stressing one's obligations toward others based upon five different relationships: ruler and subject, husband and wife, parents and children, brothers and sisters, and between friends. The ruler and subject may be considered leader and subordinate in a military unit. While communism adheres to atheism, the NLF and Lao Dong Party capitalized on the precepts of Confucianism that could be used to control individuals and even society.

The family is the most important aspect of Vietnamese culture. Individual Vietnamese lives revolve around the family, both the nuclear and the extended family. Three generations commonly live under one roof or adjacent to one another. The father is the head of the family and it is his responsibility to provide food, clothing, and shelter and make important decisions, all in accordance with the Confucian tradition. Confucian tradition holds that when someone dies their spirit lives on. Descendents will honor their ancestors, ensuring their continued goodwill. On the anniversary of a person's death ceremonies are held in his or her memory and those so honored go back three generations. Their souls are consulted before important decisions are made and to "approve" of important family occasions such as weddings, births, or buying land.

The concept of face is also extremely important to the Vietnamese and seldom understood by Westerners. It is a quality that reflects a person's reputation, prestige, and dignity, but is different from the Western

Two captured VC are guarded by a Popular Force militiaman armed with an M2 carbine. The rope is actually a means of humiliating the prisoner and did as much to keep him mentally in check as physically secured. They wear French-style khaki slouch hats and black uniforms. (Mike Holland)

concept of personal honor. Individuals, organizations, and institutions can lose or save face. Face can also be "given." A person can be given face by publicly complimenting or praising him. Accusing someone of poor performance or publicly reprimanding him will lead to loss of face. This can be done unintentionally and can be difficult to correct. To a Westerner a minor critical comment by a superior, even in public, can be shrugged off. To a Vietnamese it causes just as much loss of face and public humiliation as being publicly accused of a major blunder.

Communism

Communism demands collectivism. Therefore the individual is seen as secondary to the group, be it family, school, business, or military unit. This outlook results in strict guidelines for social interaction, intended to protect a group's face. An individual's actions can cause the group to lose face, so an individual is not just responsible for his own actions. What he does reflects on all in the collective – family or military unit.

As with any group-orientated society there are also hierarchical structures, and in Vietnam these are based on age and status. Everyone has a distinct place and role within the hierarchical structure and this worked very well for the structured nature of VC units. It applied to the three-man cell through to all unit echelons and derived from Confucianism. It places the unit leader in the role of the father responsible for making important decisions; it maintains that the individual is a part of and responsible to the collective. His failure is the unit's failure and the failure of the unit reflects on the individual.

The VC fighter, then, saw himself as a member of a hierarchical family unit, led by a father-like leader who was responsible for all decisions, who must be respected because of his seniority, and he was responsible to the unit and the unit responsible to him, promoting mutual well-being.

The rules of the party

The NLF demanded total commitment and complete sacrifice. The individual and collectives – organizations and units – were less important than the good of the whole. The party must survive and the individual

Main Force fighters cheer during a political rally. The youth of the fighters can be seen here. By 1968 the VC were largely armed with SKS carbines and some AK-47 assault rifles. Both weapons here are Type 56 carbines and assault rifles, as can be seen by the folding spike bayonets.

must give his all to it. Personal concerns, desires, and needs were considered unimportant. Security was an overriding concern. The fighters were told little, especially about planned operations. They might know that they were preparing for combat, but they knew nothing of the operation until just before its execution. Then they were only told of the task of their subunit. When relocating to another camp virtually no notice was given. They learned not to ask questions or even speculate among themselves. Rumor-mongering might be reported to the political officer.

Perhaps the most effective way to look into the VC fighter's outlook and conduct is through the rules he was to live by. The VC fighter was provided with the *Main Rules of Discipline*, which he had to commit to memory and comply with:

1. Obey all orders in your actions.
2. Do not take a single needle or piece of thread from the people.
3. Turn in everything you capture.

These rules were supplemented with the more specific *Points of Attention*. These guidelines were meant to moderate the VC's conduct and relationship with the people. When necessary, to ensure loyalty and compliance of the masses, they could be temporarily disregarded.

1. Speak politely.
2. Pay fairly for what you buy.
3. Return everything you borrow.
4. Pay for everything you damage.
5. Do not hit or swear at people.
6. Do not damage crops or property.
7. Do not take liberties with women.
8. Do not mistreat captives. (This was generally ignored.)

The *Oath of Honor* spelled out what was expected of the fighter:

1. I swear I am to sacrifice all for Vietnam. I will fight to my last breath against imperialism, colonialism, Vietnamese traitors, and

aggression in order to make Vietnam independent, democratic, and united.

2. I swear to obey absolutely all orders from my commanders, executing them wholeheartedly, promptly, and accurately.

3. I swear to fight strongly for the People without complaint and without becoming discouraged even if life is hard or dangerous. I will go forward into combat without fear and will never retreat regardless of the suffering involved.

4. I swear to learn to fight better and shape myself into a true Revolutionary soldier battling the invading American imperialists and their servants, seeking to make Vietnam democratic, wealthy, and strong.

5. I swear to preserve organizational secrecy, and to keep secret my unit's plans, the name of my unit commander, and all secrets of other revolutionary units.

6. I swear if taken by the enemy I will not reveal any information even under inhuman torture. I will remain faithful to the Revolution and not be bribed by the enemy.

7. I swear in the name of unity to love my friends in my unit as myself, to work cooperatively with them in combat and at other times.

8. I swear to maintain and protect my weapons, ensuring they are never damaged or captured by the enemy.

9. I swear that in my relationships with the People I will do three things and eschew three things. I will not steal from, threaten, nor inconvenience the People. I will do all things to win their confidence.

10. I swear to indulge in self-criticism, to be a model soldier of the Revolution, and never to harm either the Liberation Army or Vietnam.

The *Oath of the Revolutionary Soldier* was much the same as the *Oath of Honor*. The fighter committed himself to:

1. Defend the Fatherland, fight, and sacrifice myself for the People's Revolution.

2. Obey the orders received and carry out the mission of the soldier
3. Strive to improve the virtues of a Revolutionary soldier.
4. Study to improve myself and study to improve the Revolutionary Army.
5. Carry out other missions of the Revolutionary Army.
6. Be vigilant, preserve secrecy, and heighten the Revolutionary soldier's honor.
7. Help consolidate the Revolutionary Army's internal unity.
8. Preserve and save public properties.
9. Work for the solidarity between the Revolutionary Army and the People.
10. Maintain the Quality of Honor of the Revolutionary soldier.

The majority of fighters took these oaths seriously. Of course, the brutal necessities of war meant that such rules could not always be followed or were temporarily set aside. While the NLF's goal was to gain the trust and support of the people, there were many abuses and in some areas they lost or never gained that support. Brutalities and atrocities were not uncommon when it suited the VC. Indeed it was a common practice to "punish" villages for having cooperated with the government. The fact that the villagers were in no more of a position to resist giving their willing or unwilling support to government troops than they were to resisting VC incursions demanding food, taxes, and labor was generally ignored. The villagers were caught in the middle and attempted to placate whoever was making demands on them. They had no other options.

Food was often demanded by the VC. Their need for food was ravenous, not only for their immediate use, but because they stockpiled it to support passing Main Force and NVA units (ARVN troops might only steal a few chickens and vegetables for their next meal). "War taxes" were often obsessive. It was a "justification" for taking what was needed. It was seldom money – most peasants had none. War taxes might be extracted in the form of food, clothing, basic commodities, but often in labor. Villagers were assembled and quotas were assigned, for example, to produce hundreds of punji stakes, woven sleeping mats, bamboo slating and thatched roof panels for hootches, etc. Labor might also mean man and woman power to haul supplies, build fortifications, and dig tunnels. Some VC reveled in this power and took it to excesses. There were instances where VC took more than they needed and then sold or traded it in market places. Some Local Force units were known for halting buses between towns and shaking down the passengers for money, food, and even sexual favors. None of this went into NLF coffers or supply caches. They were no better than bandits.

For the believers, however, the goals of the NLF were a powerful motivation. They strongly believed that they were defending the country from an invading army bent on occupying it, that the RVN government were total puppets of the Americans, that there was an imperialistic conspiracy to make Vietnam a colony of the capitalists, and that communism would right all wrongs and give equal wealth to all. The NLF cadres visiting villages sang an enticing song. It sounded good and there was no reason not to believe them.

The VC fighter was just like any other soldier though. There were deserters, with some 80,000 surrendering to the Chieu Hoi (pronounced choo-hoy") (Open Arms) Program implemented by the RVN in 1963. VC returnees (*Hoi Chanhs*) underwent a re-education program and were paid bonuses for weapons they brought over. Some served in American units as guides and interpreters known as Kit Carson Scouts. Others, disillusioned, deserted to disappear among the local people.

The VC could be extremely valorous, even chivalrous, as well as fanatical. Many were just average young men with typical fears, weaknesses, hopes, and aspirations. There were heroes and cowards, dedicated patriots, opportunists, and some who had no idea what they were really involved in.

EXPERIENCE IN BATTLE

The average VC fighter's experience of combat would differ greatly, and some might not ever really experience any "front-line" operations. However, when they did they were often ranged against an enemy whose military might far outweighed their own. The following narrative describes such an engagement when VC fighters met US troops.

While on a routine patrol in March 1969, a VC Regional Force platoon of 24 men was moving along a low ridge overlooking a wide valley covered with rice paddies in the east. Its western end was an inundated plain of head-high elephant-grass. On the valley's south side was a thickly forested ridge with a small unseen village. The area had been peaceful and no imperialist forces had penetrated for some time. Such routine patrols were generally quite boring for the men involved.

Mao Tse Tung said, "A grain of rice is worth a drop of blood." Rice paddies covered much of Vietnam's level countryside, a factor affecting tactics. The distinct clumps of trees mark the locations of hamlets, several of which comprise a village. The nearest tree-lined fields grow other subsistence crops.

The soldiers had spent a restful night in their hammocks in an area of dense trees. The enemy never moved at night so only two guards were posted, mainly to keep one another awake during their two-hour shift. Their meager rations were cold rice balls, *nuoc mam*, and soggy noodles in tins with the tops capped by newspaper and secured with bamboo strands.

The platoon used the opportunity to practice maneuvering; training never ceased. A cell would be sent ahead to find concealed positions. They would select an unlikely spot and set up an ambush, perhaps to the flank. After waiting a while the platoon would move forward, making certain no rounds were chambered. The "ambushers" "opened fire" banging sticks together. The platoon would "return fire," maneuvering to the flanks and attempt to get behind and cut off the "enemy." It was also good practice for the ambushers – this type of meeting engagement was typical in the jungle. Whoever had the advantage of surprise would more often achieve victory. Even if the VC were outnumbered, its surprise attack and aggressive actions gave it enough advantage to break contact with minimal losses and fight another day.

However, on this day by late morning helicopters were passing over the southern ridge. The VC felt the vibrations in the air before they saw the source, and then suddenly a swarm of helicopters descended on the far west end of the ridge. More landed to the east. After several minutes they departed and it was immediately quiet – they could even hear the banging of local guerrilla gongs across the valley. They knew the villagers were moving into their hidden dugouts and tunnels. Other guerrillas would be fanning out in pairs to watch the American soldiers who had been deployed by the helicopters. Small helicopters soon began passing over in pairs, scouting. The platoon stayed in the dense trees, spreading out and attaching foliage to their rucksacks for camouflage. They knew not to look up as the helicopters passed, or even afterwards, as observers might be looking back to catch a glimpse of their rising faces. They also knew not to fire unless they were detected.

The platoon commander knew what to do. He would not await orders. The only way to communicate with the battalion was by runner, but there

A VC takes pot shots with an M1 carbine at Huey helicopters flying over. The VC were trained to fire on aircraft, but at this range the light weapon is totally ineffective.

vas no time. The American incursion would be relayed to the battalion soon enough by the guerrillas. Everyone made sure that their weapons were loaded, camouflage in place, and all equipment secured. Everyone was quiet, but resolute. It was the first time most of them would face Americans and they had heard the stories of their firepower. They moved out slowly in a dispersed formation, halting when helicopters came near. Swinging to the west they would cross the valley through the flooded elephant-grass. This would be a dangerous period, as the fighters were exposed and felt vulnerable. While the high, dense grass restricted visibility to arm's length, it provided no concealment from the air when moving. They filled their canteens from a stream and then moved into the high grass. As a helicopter approached they had to crawl through the mud and water up under the swaying grass and not move. The closer the beat

The loss of weapons caches to Free World forces sweeps was frequent and massive. In the right center are 7.62mm RPD light machine guns and lined up in the right foreground are shoulder-fired RPG-2 (B40) antitank weapons.

51

of the blades the tighter they shut their eyes. It was a slow process and they traveled in single file; if they split into squad files they would lose contact

Helicopter activity lessened as they moved slowly, but the farther they went the more separated they became. It was difficult to keep together with the starts and stops. They were most of the way across when they heard a low American voice directly in front of them. Everyone automatically halted, with a collective shudder running through them. Their senses were on high alert. They could now hear the soft sounds of men pushing through the grass.

The platoon had a B40 launcher and two M79 grenade launchers. They were positioned well forward. Their actions were automatic through long practice. The standard tactic was to barrage-fire these weapons at the enemy if contact was made. In this terrain, though, the B40 would do little good – its shells had to airburst in trees to shower those below with fragments and splinters. The commander was using hand signals to those few he could see to move them into a line facing the advancing enemy.

A long ripping burst of an AK-47 tore through the grass from the right. Firing broke out all around – repeated AK and RPD bursts, a grenade went off, and then the Americans answered, their black rifles making sharp cracks alongside the throaty bursts of M60 machine guns. The quiet thumps of grenade launchers from both sides began, followed by the muffled bangs of their impact. Red American tracers streaked through the grass. At least two fighters were hit. It was impossible to tell in the blinding grass if others were struck down. There was a sensation of urgency, awareness, but there was no time for fear (see Plate F).

Yellow smoke could be seen snaking up above the grass behind the Americans. The platoon commander and squad leaders were urging men forward, to close in with the enemy. This "belt holding" tactic was meant to hug the Americans close, even to intermingle among them in a close fight. It prevented the Americans from effectively delivering artillery and air strikes. The men pushed forward, understanding the necessity to close in.

Then they heard rotor-blades. Some of the veterans looked frantic. They continued moving forward firing short bursts, even though the American fire was increasing. At one point a half dozen grenades were showered on them with thumping blasts, spraying mud and water. More fighters went down.

The helicopters grew louder, and one was coming straight at them. White streaks of smoke burst from it. They could hear Americans shouting what sounded like warnings. There were puffs of red smoke then buzzing drones as a giant scythe swung through the grass. Now there was fear.

The dead and wounded were peppered with nail-like darts. The helicopter was coming back around. The Americans were firing full-automatic

A dead Main Force fighter with his personal effects scattered after being searched for items of intelligence value. Some 7.62mm AK cartridges have been spilled from a cloth bag in which spare ammunition was carried. Unless the man served in a Local Force unit, or news was eventually carried by comrades in Main Force units, the next of kin were never notified by the NLF or PLA.

bursts and their shouts showed they were advancing. The survivors were moving to the left away from the American sweep in a collective rush to flee the horror. More rockets streaked in, this time detonating in massive blasts, showering water and throwing up big clumps of grass and mud, as well as men, across the valley. The fighters crawled up under the grass and kept crawling. Helicopters constantly beat overhead, firing more rockets and spraying machine guns.

The fighters crawled until the sounds were dim. They lay exhausted in the water. The sun beat down on the grass, baking them in the mud. Red ants swarmed over them and leeches attacked. They choked down rice balls and drank the last of their water. There was little talk – each man kept his thoughts to himself, embarrassed and angry at how they had fled leaving their comrades behind.

Night fell and clouds of mosquitoes reinforced the ants. They began moving again, with whispered shouts and low whistles. There were 16 accounted for, seven wounded, two unable to walk. It was a struggle to carry the injured through the thick grass. Once back at the ridge they cut poles to sling hammocks for the wounded and rotated carrying them and their weapons and equipment. Sometime before dawn one of the wounded, a popular machine gunner, died. They took time to bury him, scraping out a shallow hole, and pressed on. It was an exhausting all-night march. Flashlights were used owing to their fear of snakes.

They staggered into the base camp after breakfast. The out guards met them and sent word to the camp. Comrades rushed to them, helping the wounded to the aid station. One of the men had to have his hand amputated. In a proper medical facility it would have been saved, but their makeshift aid was more like 19th-century care. The seriously wounded were given caffeine IVs as a stimulant. There was nothing for pain other than black-market aspirin. They were given food, and comrades wanted to know everything that had happened. No one wanted to talk about it. The platoon commander reported to the company commander; they and the company political officer reported to the battalion commander.

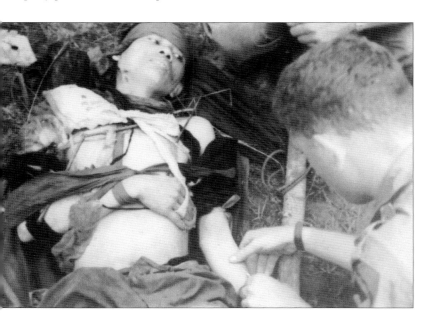

A VC suffering multiple wounds receives treatment from an American medic. Medical care available to the VC was crude at best.

That night a self-criticism session was held with the company and battalion commanders and political officers present. It was a difficult time for all. There was a great deal of concern over the numbers of dead and possibly wounded left behind. Most equipment of the nine dead or captured had been left and only four weapons were recovered. Morale was low. Policy was to remove the dead from the battlefield so that the enemy would not know the extent of casualties, or pose the bodies for humiliating victory photos, and collect intelligence from documents. There was another reason. The Vietnamese feel strongly about a proper burial – death is not the end, but is the final stage where one's life is transformed into another. If one is mutilated or the body lost and unburied its soul will wander without finding peace. During assaults the VC used scaling ladders and hooks and ropes to drag the dead from the battlefield.

The self-criticism session and battle critique was as much an effort to learn from their actions and reinforce their morale as to determine what mistakes were made. The commanders knew what such overwhelming firepower could do. It was a week before the platoon was called to patrol again. Replacements did not arrive for over a month and then only five men came.

Apart from instances like this, VC units actually saw comparatively little action. Other than skirmishes, chance patrol contacts, and occasional harassing actions, major engagements were rare, often only two or three a year. Therefore a great deal of planning went into operations to ensure that the participants were really prepared. Once a major operation was proposed, such as an attack on a firebase or convoy ambush, many planning options were considered. Ammunition and supplies were built up – ammunition expenditure would be massive and a unit could not be left with low stocks after the operation was completed. Political considerations and effects were studied and the provincial central committee was just as involved with the plan as the military headquarters. Six months' preparation preceded some operations, although others required much less, even just a few weeks. Of course, targets of opportunity were also attacked if resources allowed. Free World forces learned that if they stayed in one place for three days they were inviting attack. The VC observed for a day. On the second and third days they

Here is a hired Vietnamese demonstrator working on a US Army post to help familiarize US soldiers with VC tactics and techniques. Emerging from a tunnel, he is armed with a Chinese-made Type 56 (AK-47) assault rifle. Type 56s were found with detachable or folding spike bayonets. Soviet AK-47s did not have folding bayonets.

econnoitered and conducted rehearsals. They
attacked on the last night.

A doctrine memoir aide "four quicks, one slow, and three strongs" was followed in a logical sequence: slow plan (lengthy preparation), quick advance (movement to the objective from a safe distance away), quick attack (rapid surprise attack), strong fight (violence of action), strong assault (concentrated attack), strong pursuit (follow-up attack and consolidation on the objective), quick clearance (collect captured materials, move off the objective), and quick withdraw (disengage and depart the area before enemy support arrives).

Special Attack Corps

Occasionally units were asked to provide volunteers for special assignments. At other times individuals were recommended for such assignments by commanders and political officers, interviewed and then asked to volunteer. An extremely important organization to the VC/NVA was the Special Attack Corps (Bo Tu Linh Dac Cong). These highly trained and dedicated troops were known as "sappers" to Free World forces. They are usually thought of as commandos – highly skilled at infiltrating through barbed wire and other obstacles and executing swift, deadly attacks on installations. Functionally, they can be described as reconnaissance-commandos.

Sappers were employed as a less costly alternative to mass assaults with huge losses of conventional fighters. They were trained to operate in small groups, stealthily infiltrating through obstacles and neutralizing Claymore mines, booby traps, and trip flares. Using the cover of darkness they would creep into an installation and silently move to their targets rather than charging. Command posts, fire direction centers, communications centers, artillery positions, ammunition and fuel dumps, troop quarters, parked aircraft, etc. were their key targets, what they called "going for the guts." In a sense sappers were the VC/NVA's precision artillery, albeit hand-delivered. Another primary mission was reconnaissance and they

VC rocket artillery battalions were armed with the Soviet 122mm DKB. The launcher had an 11,000-yard (10,000m) range. It could be broken down into man-pack loads. Simple wooden launch troughs and even earth ramps were also used to launch the rockets.

A Chieu Hoi (Open Arms) sapper demonstrates how they were trained to slip quietly through the densest of barriers, spring-steel concertina razor wire in this instance.

undertook a wide variety of intelligence collection missions ranging from reconnoitering routes for larger units and keeping Free World installations under surveillance, through to map making.

Sapper volunteers underwent up to six months' training at special schools in the south. Many, however, received only a few weeks or even days of initial training before undertaking a mission. Survivors went through additional training. They operated in 12–15-man sections (*phan dot*), typically three to a company (*dai doe dac cong*). The hallmark of their missions was detailed reconnaissance, precise planning and coordination, rehearsals, surprise, and extremely violent quick action.

Rather than the usual weeks spent planning an attack, only days were allotted to prepare for a rushed mission. Not even the usual "farewell party" was held. One such occasion was when the VC discovered that the Americans had established a temporary firebase atop a steep-sided hill. Four 105mm howitzers had been brought in by helicopter. The base was defended only by a rifle company. Including the artillerymen, there were fewer than 170 Americans on the hill. The VC's timing was crucial as the Americans could leave at any time.

Sapper cells approached as close as they could to the base's perimeter, but the hillside was bomb- and shell-blasted bare except for shattered tree trunks and limbs, rocks, and crumbling soil; a difficult climb under fire. Forced to remain down-slope, the reconnaissance cell could not determine the base's layout. However, it was surrounded, by only a double-stacked coil of concertina wire with Claymores and trip flares. The real danger was artillery from neighboring firebases.

Two sapper sections of ten and 12 men moved silently up the hillside and penetrated from the north and northwest. For the past three nights the firebase had been mortared two or three times. The VC arranged another session of mortar fire to provide cover for their sappers; this would begin at 0400 hours. Each section would cut two gaps in the wire. A four-man cell from each section would attempt to enter the base. Two Main Force companies were prepared to launch an assault, one through each pair of gaps, as soon as the sappers' demolition charges began to

VC assault troops fight their way up a hillside toward an ARVN position. Supporting mortar, recoilless rifle, machine-gun, and RPG fire would be directed on the position even as the assault troops stormed into it. This is probably a staged shot, as few assaults were executed in daylight.

explode or when they were detected by the Americans. A third company was in reserve to follow one of the other companies on order or to cover their withdrawal. Two recoilless rifles on an adjacent hill, and a mortar platoon, would begin firing into the base once the attack was launched, irrespective of the presence of their own attacking fighters.

The sappers were already moving when the first mortar rounds struck. As smoke and dust rolled down the hillside they reached the wire. One sapper clipped wire ties securing the concertina to steel pickets. Another, stripped to his shorts and greased, slid through the coils, inserting safety pins in trip flares to lock their arming levers. He clipped the electrical firing wires of two Claymores. A bamboo scaling ladder was slid under the coils. Its outward end was propped up by Y-sticks. A sapper slithered under the ladder as far as he could go; then pushing up with his shoulders raised it and inserted two more Y-sticks. The grenade and demolition charge-armed sappers wiggled though the "tunnel." All the while mortar rounds detonated loudly in the base. Illumination flares fired from another firebase drifted over, casting an ever-changing crisscross pattern of shadows through the wire and dust.

The first sappers through the wire ran, crouching low, at the dark lumps of sandbags representing perimeter bunkers. Muzzle flashes immediately blossomed and red tracers streaked through the wire, cutting down sappers. Some made it through and rushed toward the donut-like artillery positions to be met with rifle fire and grenades. Each sandbagged position was a miniature fortress. One sapper chucked a 15lb (6.8kg) satchel charge into a position followed by a deafening explosion. The howitzer's tires were shredded, its sight damaged, and some of the crew killed and wounded, but the gun was still serviceable. The supporting 75mm recoilless rifles on the adjacent hill were cracking rounds into the hilltop, mortars and grenades thumped, small arms rattled, and the hillside and adjacent hills were blasted by artillery from two other

Fighters assault past a 7.62mm SGM (Type 57) heavy machine gun. This weapon had a solid, stable mount, making it a good fire support weapon. They were often positioned on dominating ground several hundred yards away from a Free World outpost to provide suppressive fire. Note the fluted barrel. The SG-43 (Type 53) had a smooth barrel. (Central Press/Getty Images)

firebases. The din and confusion were unimaginable. The assault companies never made it up the hillside. The sappers were on their own.

It was over by dawn. The battered hilltop fortress was still in American hands, having suffered fewer than two-dozen casualties. A replacement sight and tires were flown in for the damaged howitzer a couple of hours later with an ammunition resupply and hot chow. Most of the sappers were found with their blasted remains scattered through the wire. Others lay crumpled between the artillery positions. Two were found wounded and unconscious. The Americans buried the bodies without ceremony in shallow holes where they lay. The next day the howitzers were airlifted out to establish a new base as the infantry they were supporting moved on.

AFTERMATH OF BATTLE

All VC/NVA prisoners of war, regardless of who captured them, were turned over to the ARVN. The thousands captured were placed in re-indoctrination programs of varying effectiveness. Few were released during the war.

With the North Vietnamese victory on April 30, 1975, the surviving PLA fighters and officials of the NLF, with its in-place local government and officials tagged for national government positions, soon faced a bitter realization. The NLF, PLA, and PRG played little role in the victory and its leaders had been misled by Hanoi into thinking that they would participate in the new order. They had been bled dry during the Tet Offensive and were a shadow of their former selves, with Main Force units largely manned by NVA fillers, as were all leadership positions. NLF/PRG officials were stunned to find the VC divisions were absorbed into the NVA. During the great Saigon victory parade only a few small rag-tag VC units followed behind the NVA divisions. The final role played by the PRG was to serve as a sham transitory government and sign the instrument of unification between the North and South to create the Socialist Republic of Vietnam on June 2, 1976.

Former VC returnees (*Hoi Chanhs*) in the Chieu Hoi Program participate in a government re-indoctrination session. Captured VC prisoners of war underwent similar re-indoctrination, but few were released.

NLF/PRG officials were reassigned to local government jobs and many were simply retired. The thousands of VC prisoners held by the Saigon government had expected to be released and welcomed as heroes, with some desire to return to the armed forces. Instead they were moved to different camps and endured months of new re-indoctrination programs before discharge. Many were ineligible for any kind of compensation by the new government. What has so long been claimed as a civil war to reunify a country proved only to be a war of expansionism and domination by the communist North.

COLLECTIONS, MUSEUMS, AND REENACTMENT

Numerous US Army museums display Vietnam War collections with VC/NVA equipment and weapons. These include the museums of the remaining active duty divisions which served in Vietnam: 1st Infantry (Ft. Riley, KS), 4th Infantry (Ft. Hood, TX), 25th Infantry (Schofield Barracks, HI), 82d Airborne (Ft. Bragg, NC), 101st Airborne (Ft. Campbell, KY), 1st Cavalry Division (Ft. Hood). Most Army posts have a Vietnam display in their museum or historical holding area. Posts with branch museums all have significant Vietnam displays. The National Infantry Museum at Ft. Benning, GA, and the US Military Academy Museum at West Point, NY, possess excellent Vietnam collections. The National Vietnam War Museum site in Mineral Wells, TX (near Dallas), was dedicated in 2004, but will not open for some years yet. Some of the best collections are in civilian collector hands, however.

The collecting of Vietnam memorabilia is a major field, the artifacts ranging from mementos, uniforms, and equipment to insignia. Collectors are strongly urged to use caution and question the authenticity of any item presented as authentic Vietnam era, especially VC/NVA items. Replicas made in Vietnam, elsewhere in Asia, and in the US are often sold as authentic at a high cost.

There are significant numbers of Vietnam reenactor groups, not just representing US forces but Australian too, in the United States and

A collection of early captured VC arms, among which are a .30-cal. M1 carbine, two French 7.5mm MAS Mle. 36 rifles, 8mm Label Mle. 1886 rifles, and a few other assorted arms. Of more importance are the various documents, which include unit rosters, ammunition and arms issue accounts, and supplies records. (Mike Holland)

other countries. Internet searches will turn up many. To oppose these groups there are a surprising number of VC/NVA reenactor units. Replica VC/NVA uniforms and equipment are available at reasonable prices. Since the VC used much locally fabricated gear it is easy for reenactors to make their own authentic-looking gear. In the United States, semi-automatic AK-47s are available, while SKS and M1944 carbines can be purchased at a comparatively low cost. Furthermore, just about any US weapon from World War II through 1970 may be used, as well as a variety of foreign weapons of the same era.

BIBLIOGRAPHY

Chanoff, David and Doan van Toai, *Portrait of the Enemy*, Random House, New York (1986)

Conley, Michael C., *The Communist Insurgent Infrastructure in South Vietnam: A Study of Organization and Strategy*, Headquarters, Department of the Army, DA Pamphlet 550-106, Washington, DC (1967)

Dudman, Richard, *40 Days with the Enemy: The Story of a Journalist Held Captive by Guerrillas in Cambodia*, Liveright, New York, (1971)

Emering, Edward J., *Weapons and Field Gear of the North Vietnamese and Viet Cong*, Schiffer Publishing, Atglen, PA (1998)

Katallo, Dennis C. and Allen J. Bending, *North Vietnamese Army/Viet Cong Uniforms and Field Equipment 1965–75*, Miltec Enterprises, Addison, IL (1988)

Lanning, Michael Lee and Dan Cragg, *Inside the VC and the NVA: The Real Story of North Vietnam's Armed Forces*, Ballantine Books, New York (1992)

Lulling, Darrel R., *Communist Militaria of the Vietnam War*, Revised Edition, M.C.N. Press, Tulsa, OK (1980)

Mangold, Tom, *The Tunnels of Cu Chi*, Presidio Press, Novato, CA (1986)

McCoy, James W., *Secrets of the Viet Cong*, Hippocrene Books, New York (1992) (Little on VC, focus is on NVA.)

Pike, Douglas, *Viet Cong: The Organization and Techniques of the National Liberation Front of South Vietnam*, MIT Press, Cambridge, MA (1966)

Stanton, Shelby L., *Vietnam Order of Battle: A Complete Illustrated Reference to U.S. Army Combat and Support Forces in Vietnam 1961–1973*, Stackpole Books, Mechanicsburg, PA (2003)

Truong Nhu Tang, *A Viet Cong Memoir: An Inside Account of the Vietnam War and its Aftermath*, Vintage Books, New York (1986)

Webb, Kate, *On the Other Side: 28 Days with the Viet Cong*, Quadrangle Books, New York (1972)

COLOR PLATE COMMENTARY

A: TRAINING AND INDOCTRINATION

Political indoctrination was just as much a part of training in the VC as were weapons and tactics. The lower the level, the more political education the fighters received. Recruits for the Village Defense Forces were taken into the jungle to a temporary camp and given only a week or so of rudimentary combat training heavily laced with indoctrination by Local Force or Mobile Force cadre. Combat training mainly consisted of weapons instruction in which recruits would fire a few rounds. Much of the instruction was by lecture and was often repetitive. Real training came from on-the-job experience. Here a cadreman instructs recruits on the operation of the Soviet-made 7.62mm M1944 carbine. The canvas cartridge pouches were intended for four SKS carbine ten-round stripper clips. There were no uniforms or equipment – the fighters were expected to obtain or make their own.

B: VILLAGE DEFENSE AND LOCAL FORCES

Village Defense and Local Forces wore the "uniform" of the peasant farmer, not only to blend into the population by shedding their minimal military gear, but to be identifiable with the people (1 and 2). Abandoning their spartan gear was no great loss, but they would make efforts to hide their valuable weapons for later recovery. Individual equipment was austere, often homemade, and included discards from transiting NVA units, or gear pilfered or speciously purchased from local government units. Such local forces did not need much. They seldom strayed out overnight and returned to their village after completing their patrols. Here the VC fighter's weapon is the Russian-made 7.62mm Mosin-Nagant M1944 carbine with an integral folding spike bayonet (3). The Chinese version was the Type 53. The M1944 used the same 7.62x54mm ammunition as Soviet machine guns, but was loaded in five-round stripper clips. Plain bulleted Type L ball ammunition was the most common (3a), but yellow-tipped Type D heavy ball rounds were also used (3b). His company would probably have a few 7.62mm Simonov SKS carbines, here a Chinese-made Type 56 with a folding spike bayonet (4); Soviet SKSs had blade bayonets. The SKS used the same shorter 7.62x39mm cartridge as the AK-47 assault rifle, but issued in ten-round stripper clips (4a). 7.62x54mm rifle and

Water buffalo carts were used to haul supplies. The high wheels and the substantial power of the water buffaloes allowed the carts to be drawn though deep mud. Civilians volunteered or were threatened into manning the carts.

machine-gun ammunition was issued in boxes that contained two 300-round galvanized cans with a key and tear strip (5). The rugged French 9mm MaT-49 submachine guns (6) was still in use, its folding magazine housing and telescoping stock making it ideal to conceal. Some leather MaT-49 pouches for two magazines survived (6a). A form of simple haversack (7), here of Eastern European manufacture, might be carried containing ammunition, rice balls for the midday meal (7a), a sheet of green plastic for a rain cape, a length of cord, matches and cigarette makings, a homemade knife as a utility tool (7b), and one or two locally fabricated grenades. An old scrounged NVA canteen (8), which came in many varieties like this plastic model colored light and dark green, tan, and purple, might be carried in the haversack as its web straps had deteriorated. Ingenuity and need led to such items as a Coca Cola bottle rigged as a canteen with a wooden stopper and carrying cord (9). Also seen here is the little-used VC hat and fiber helmet badge (10).

C: JUNGLE GRENADE FACTORY

A great deal of a Local Force fighter's time was spent constructing base camps, bunkers, tunnels, and in some areas maintaining weapons and equipment and fabricating booby traps. Such work was commonly conducted in small hidden camps some distance from the base village. This reduced the chance of discovery, as villages were frequently searched by government and Free World forces. Everyone was given jobs. Here, expended American M18 colored smoke grenades are remanufactured into explosive grenades. The bottom is cut out and the burnt smoke compound residue scraped out. The expended fuse is removed and rebuilt using a .22-cal. cartridge with the bullet and propellant removed, inserted as an igniter cap, and fitted with a short length of time fuse with a blasting cap crimped on. Safety levers and arming pins were also recovered for reuse. The body is filled with captured C4 or a 1/2lb (0.23kg) TNT block with nails or gravel for fragmentation. A wooden disc is cut to plug the bottom. Even cruder grenades were fabricated from soft-drink and beer cans. Efficient assembly lines were set up to fabricate such expedient weapons. Sometimes different steps of construction were undertaken at different camps and the components transported between them by loyal civilians. The author's camp strike force employed a former VC armorer who taught the author the production steps. We fabricated a half-dozen such grenades in one leisurely afternoon and they worked quite well. The armorer said an experienced production line of ten men and women could turn out over 100 grenades a day … so long as the Americans kept supplying grenade bodies, which VC fighters were ordered to search for, along with other useable materials after Free World units departed an area.

D: AMBUSH

Ambush was one of the most common and preferred methods of attack. It allowed a relatively smaller force to attack a larger and more mobile enemy. The key to a successful ambush was, of course, complete surprise. The positions of the ambush force had to be extremely well concealed and dug-in for protection from not only the Free World force's own heavy firepower, but also from the

ARVN Rangers stand guard over VC prisoners and captured weapons, ammunition, and equipment during the 1968 Tet Offensive in Saigon. The Ranger to the right is armed with a .45-cal. M3A1 submachine gun and the man to the left ha a 5.56mm M16A1 rifle. Both weapons were employed by th VC. (Central Press/Getty Images)

artillery, attack helicopters, and fighter-bombers that woul soon arrive. Positions were often dug the night before Leaders would personally assign each man his positio and sector of fire, with particular attention given to th positioning of machine guns and antivehicle weapons RPGs and recoilless rifles. Here Main Force soldiers prepar a 7.62mm RPD light machine-gun position. Position were camouflaged all round as well as overhead. Nort Vietnamese (copied from a French design and shown here Chinese, and American entrenching tools were used. Ric sickles were used to cut vegetation, which was replaced a soon as it began wilting. One fighter wears canvas an rubber Canadian-made Bata boots captured from the CID(The camouflage cape made from parachute nylon wa draped over the shoulders and rucksack. Rucksacks wer left at rally points in the rear to allow a quick withdrawal.

E: MAIN FORCE

VC Main Force (1 and 2) and to a lesser extent, Mobile Forc troops were more abundantly equipped and armed tha Local Forces. Much of the equipment and armament wa of Chinese origin, but Soviet, other Warsaw Pact, an captured Free World gear and weapons were also used This fighter wears a black and white checkered scar

A wide variety of colors were worn, often used as friend-or-foe recognition. The 7.62mm Soviet AK-47 (3) and Chinese Type 56 assault rifles were virtually symbols of the VC. This example is Soviet-made and lacks an integral folding spike bayonet found on some Chinese models. Main and Mobile Forces lived out of their rucksacks (4) carrying everything they needed to live for extended periods: rations, extra clothing, mosquito net, hammock, and plastic sheet for a ground cloth or rain shelter. Designs with both two and three pockets were issued from North Vietnamese and Chinese sources, made in various shades of green and tan. The CIDG rucksack was copied from the three-pocket North Vietnamese design, which in turn was copied from a French model. It is difficult to determine if particular web gear items were made in North Vietnam or China. Markings were few, usually limited to numbers, and most Chinese gear made for the NVA/VC was of a different and cheaper design than the Chinese used themselves. Chinese ideographs will be found on some items. Chinese entrenching tools (5) came with heavy leather carriers (5a), though these quickly deteriorated. The Chinese-designed three-pocket AK chest pouches (6) were popular. The four smaller side pockets held an oiler, cleaning gear, and clipped ammunition. Four types of oilers are displayed (6a) – these were also marked with the Russian letters "A" (cleaning solvent) and "O" (lubricating oil). The SKS carbine was provided with Chinese Type 67 ten-pocket waist pouches (7). Another type used tie-tapes instead of wooden toggles and loops. Each pocket held two ten-round stripper clips for a total of 200 rounds. Several types of canteens were issued. This aluminum Chinese canteen (8) was provided with a web strap carrier while 9 is the same Chinese design, but with a North Vietnamese-made belt carrier cover. Troops sometimes etched their names or artwork on the sides of aluminum canteens with a knife point. Two-pocket grenade carriers (10) were provided either with a shoulder strap or two belt loops on the back. Chinese Type 59 stick grenades are carried. There was also a scarcer four-pocket version. French-style mess kits were sometimes issued, but a simple enameled rice bowl with chopsticks (11) was the most common mess gear. When moving long distances a rice bag (12) might be carried draped around the shoulders behind the neck. They held up to 15lb 5oz (7kg) of rice in a tan, brown, green, or white light cotton tube.

F: FIREFIGHT

The unexpected engagement was the most common form of firefight experienced by the VC. Such contacts were chance encounters. Whoever detected the approaching enemy first, even just seconds before the other, held an advantage. But at short ranges, as were so often encountered in close terrain, that advantage could melt away in moments owing to one side or the other making the right decisions to deploy and establish fire superiority. The VC knew that they had only minutes to overwhelm the Free World forces or break contact before artillery, gunships, and fighter-bombers arrived. If they chose to fight it out they moved in so close that the Free World forces could not bring their firepower assets to bear directly on them. The VC often extended their flanks, looking for the enemy's exposed flank. These Main Force fighters are armed with an AK-47 assault rifle, a .30-cal. M2 carbine, RPG-2 (B40) antitank

weapons, and 40mm M79 grenade launcher. (See Osprey Warrior 98: *US Army Infantryman in Vietnam*, Plate F for the other side of the firefight.)

G: SAPPERS

The mission of sappers required specialized weapons and equipment. Much of this they had to fabricate themselves and they demonstrated a great deal of imagination. Never before or since have such detailed and elaborate techniques been developed for breaching the extensive barriers and protective measures of military installations. Often sappers operated wearing nothing more than shorts and socks to protect the feet (1); this man is unarmed except for a crude homemade wire-cutter (3), and stiff wire double-ended hooks (4) were used to spread cut spring steel concertina wire. Heavy rubber bands on his wrist were to hold down the arming levers of trip flares and booby-trapped grenades. Other sappers were more fully uniformed (2), here with a US Army undershirt and NVA trousers and shoes. He is armed with a 7.62mm North Vietnamese modified Type 50 ("K50M") submachine gun (Soviet PPSh-41 with the barrel jacket cut back, an AK-47 pistol grip, and a French MaT-49 telescoping stock) (5). He has a three-pocket pouch for its 35-round magazines (6). He also carries a Soviet RKG-3, which has a shaped-charge antitank grenade (7) that could penetrate concrete and sandbag bunkers. All types of hand grenades were used to attack targets and exposed personnel. Satchel charges were fabricated by packing Soviet (8) and Chinese (9) 1lb 2oz (1kg) TNT charges into sandbags or other small packs (7oz/200g charges were half as thick). Pole charges (10) were fitted with many forms of demolitions or, as here, four Chinese "pineapple" fragmentation stick grenades. These were shoved into firing ports, doorways, windows, or set against aircraft. Board or bamboo scaling ladders were used to climb over barbed-wire barriers or were shoved under barriers and propped up with "Y" sticks, allowing sappers to crawl under the wire. Ladders were also used as litters to carry off casualties.

H: PRISONER OF WAR

The ultimate fear for the VC, besides death, was capture. More VC were captured while being rounded up as suspects in sweeps by government and Free World troops than were actually captured in combat. The VC would often go down fighting rather than endure capture. Their treatment varied considerably depending on whom they were captured by and the circumstances. In the heat of combat, odds were against considerate treatment. On the other hand there was a fair chance that their wounds were urgently treated, if nothing else to keep them alive for interrogation. This severely wounded sapper wears a captured US camouflage jacket, not an uncommon occurrence. Enemy POWs captured by the Americans and other Free World forces were turned over to the Vietnamese. They were interrogated at one of 18 Combined Interrogation Centers and held in POW camps throughout the country under reasonable but tough conditions. There they underwent political re-indoctrination. Because of this, with the 1975 fall of the Republic of Vietnam, they were forced to undergo communist re-indoctrination under even harsher conditions. The new rulers of the South had little use for former VC.

INDEX

References to illustrations are shown in **bold**. Plates are shown with page and caption locators in brackets.

ambushes 50, **50**, 62, **D** (36, 62)
appearance 18–20
  female VC **14**
  local auxiliaries **59**
  Main Forces 19–20, **45–47**, **D–F** (36–38, 62–63)
  Special Attack Corps 63, **G** (39, 63)
  Village Defense Forces 19, 61, **B** (34, 61–62)
artillery *see* weapons and artillery
ARVN (Army of the Republic of Vietnam) **4**, 12, 21, 41–42, **62**
assaults **20**, **42**, 55–58, **56–57**
atrocities 13

battalions 9
battle experience 48–58, 62, 63, **D** (36, 62), **F** (38, 63)
belief and belonging 44–49
booby traps **27**, 41, 43, **43**

cadres 9–10
Cambodia 7
camps 32, **47**
casualties
  burial 54
  notification of next of kin 52
cell structure 31
China: help for VC 20–21
CIDG (Civilian Irregular Defense Group) 42
collections 59
communications *see* radios
communism 45
companies 9
Confucianism 44–45

dead and death **52**, 54
deserters 48–49, **58**
divisions 9

equipment 26–30, 62, 63, **B** (34, 61–62), **D–E** (36–37, 62–63)
  canteens **27**, 63, **E** (37, 62–63)
  entrenching tools **5**, 28, 63, **E** (37, 62–63)
  mess gear **27**, 63, **E** (37, 62–63)
  plastic sheets 28, 62, **B** (34, 61–62)
  rucksacks and haversacks 28, 62, 63, **B** (34, 61–62), **E** (37, 62–63)
  Special Attack Corps 63, **G** (39, 63)
  webgear 26–27, 63, **E** (37, 62–63)

face, losing or saving 44–45, **45**
family: attitudes to 44
field fortifications **50**
  digging **9**
firefights 52–53, 63, **F** (38, 63)
firing positions **50**
food 41, 48, **49**, 50
French Indochina: division 6
furniture **47**

GPA (Guerrilla Popular Army; Local Forces) 10, 19

see also Village Defense Forces
guard duty 30–31

haircuts 18
helicopters **16**, **51**
Ho Chi Minh 6
Ho Chi Minh Trail **21**
honor and humiliation 44–45, **45**

indoctrination 17, **17**, 61, **A** (33, 61)

Lao Dong Party 5, 7
leisure 41
Local Forces *see* GPA
logistics 20, **21**, 48, **61**

Main Forces
  appearance 19–20, **45–47**, 62–63, **D–F** (36–38, 62–63)
  at firing positions **50**
  organization 8–9
  unit HQ **29**
medals and awards 41
medical care 43–44, 53, **53**
morality 41, 44
museums 59

NLF (National Liberation Front)
  aims and activities 6–7
  background 5
  party rules 45–48
  see also Viet Cong
North Vietnam
  after the war 58, 59
  aims 6
NVA (North Vietnamese Army) 4–5, 7, 9, 58

oaths 46–48
organization 8–10, 31

patrols 31, 32–41, 49–50
pay 41
People's Liberation Army *see* Viet Cong
People's Revolutionary Party *see* PRP
PF (Popular Force) 12, 31–32, 42, **45**
  outpost **32**
PLA (People's Liberation Army) *see* Viet Cong
planning **30**, 54–55
PRG (Provisional Revolutionary Government) 7, 58–59
prisoners of war **45**, 58, 59, **62**, 63, **H** (40, 63)
PRP (People's Revolutionary Party) 6–7

radios 16, **16**, **29**, 30
rail system **6**
razor wire **55**
RDC (Rural Development Cadre) 11–12
recruitment 11–14
reenactment 59–60
Regional Forces (VC) 9, 32–41
RF (Regional Forces; South Vietnamese militia) 12, 42
rice paddies **49**
Rural Development Cadre *see* RDC

salvage teams 42–44, 62
sandals 19, **19**

sappers *see* Special Attack Corps
self-criticism 17, 54
service conditions 30–44
shouters 31–32
smoke screens **42**
Soviet Union: help for VC 21
Special Attack Corps (sappers) 55–58, **55**, 63, **G** (39, 63)

taxes, war 48
Tet Offensive (1968) **5**
training 14–17, **15–17**, 61, **A** (33, 61)

US Army
  battle experience 50–53
  local attitudes to 12
  VC attitude to 42

Viet Cong (VC; PLA; military arm of NLF)
  after the war 58–59
  background 4–5
  ethnic groups included 18
  and NVA 5, 7, 9, 58
  qualities and faults 5
  real name 5
  suspects **11**, **59**
  US nicknames for 5
Village Defense Forces 10, 19, 30–32, 61–62, **B** (34, 61–62)

water buffalo carts **61**
weapons and artillery 20–26
  ammunition 25, **52**, 61–62, **B** (34, 61–62)
  carbines
    M1 **14–15**, 23, **24**, **51**, **60**
    M2 23, **45**, 63, **F** (38, 63)
    M1944 **61**, **A–B** (33–34, 61–62)
    Type 56 (SKS) **42**, **46**, 61, **B** (34, 61–62)
  grenade launchers 23, 63, **F** (38, 63)
  grenades
    antitank 63, **G** (39, 63)
    hand 25, **25**, **29**, 62, 63, **C** (35, 62), **E** (37, 62–63)
    rifle 18
  homemade handguns 23
  machine guns
    German **22**
    heavy **5**, **57**
    RPD light **20**, 25, **51**, 62, **D** (36, 62)
    sub 23, **27**, **29**, 62, 63, **B** (34, 61–62), **G** (39, 63)
  mortars 26
  pistols 25
  repairs **28**
  rifles 23–24
    AK-47s **20**, 24–25, **25**, **46**, **54**, 63, **E–F** (37–38, 62–63)
    automatic 23–24
    M16A1 **62**
    Mle. **60**
    recoilless **24**, 26, **28**
  rocket launchers **55**
  RPG antitank weapons 25, **26**, **51**, 63, **F** (38, 63)
  satchel and pole charges 63, **G** (39, 63)
  VC manufacture 43–44, **43–44**
women: in the VC 13–14, **14–15**